sion, is analyzed in its relation to the property tax.

This thorough, constructive coverage of the property tax will be valuable to economists as well as to officials of state and local government. Editor Arthur D. Lynn, Jr., is Professor of Economics and Law and Associate Dean of Faculties at Ohio State University.

Part I. An Overview: *The Institutional Context of Property Tax Administration,* Arthur D. Lynn, Jr. *Is the Property Tax Conceptually and Practically Administrable?* Harold M. Groves.

Part II. Administrative Organization: *Potential for Organizational Improvement of Property Tax Administration,* Kenneth C. Back. *The Effect of Electronic Data Processing upon Property Tax Administration,* John D. Cole II. *Improved Property Tax Administration: Legislative Opportunities and Probabilities,* Paul V. Corusy.

Part III. Assessment Procedures: *An Evaluation of Self-Assessment under a Property Tax,* Daniel M. Holland and William M. Vaughn. *Valuation of Property Interests for Ad Valorem Taxation of Extractive Industry and Agricultural Realty: Problems and Solutions,* Anthony G. Ferraro. *Assessment of Land in Urban/Rural Fringe Areas,* Frederick D. Stocker. *Some Observations on Property Tax Valuation and the Significance of Full Value Assessment,* Henry Aaron. *Assessment Standards: Highest and Best Use as a Basis for Land Appraisal and Assessment,* A. M. Woodruff.

Part IV. Administration and Evolving Property Tax Policy: *Property Tax Administration and Hawaii's Land Use Law,* Shelley M. Mark. *Property Taxation: Policy Potentials and Probabilities,* Ronald B. Welch.

A Conference Discussion, moderated by Paul E. Alyea, concludes the book.

The Property Tax and Its Administration

Proceedings of a symposium
Sponsored by the

COMMITTEE ON TAXATION, RESOURCES,
AND ECONOMIC DEVELOPMENT (TRED)

at the
University of Wisconsin—Milwaukee
1967

THE
PROPERTY
TAX and Its
Administration

Edited by
Arthur D. Lynn, Jr.

THE UNIVERSITY OF WISCONSIN PRESS
Madison, Milwaukee, and London
1969

Published by
The University of Wisconsin Press
Box 1379, Madison, Wisconsin 53701
The University of Wisconsin Press, Ltd.
27–29 Whitfield Street, London, W.1

Printed in the United States of America by
Kingsport Press, Inc., Kingsport, Tennessee

Standard Book Number 299–05210–9
Library of Congress Catalog Card Number 69–16110

Contributors

Henry Aaron
Economist, Council of Economic Advisors

Kenneth C. Back
Finance Officer, Government of the District of Columbia

John D. Cole II
Vice President, Cole-Layer-Trumble Company

Paul V. Corusy
Executive Director, International Association of Assessing Officers

Anthony G. Ferraro
Director of Appraisals, Colorado Tax Commission—State of Colorado

Harold M. Groves
Professor of Economics, University of Wisconsin

Daniel M. Holland
Professor of Finance, Sloan School of Management, Massachusetts Institute of Technology

Arthur D. Lynn, Jr.
Professor of Economics and Law and Associate Dean of Faculties, The Ohio State University

Shelley M. Mark
Director, Department of Economic Development and Planning— State of Hawaii

Frederick D. Stocker
Professor of Business Research, The Ohio State University

William M. Vaughn
Department of Economics, Massachusetts Institute of Technology

Ronald B. Welch
Assistant Executive Secretary, Property Taxes, State Board of Equalization—State of California

A. M. Woodruff
Chancellor, University of Hartford

Conference Discussants

Paul E. Alyea, Chairman
Emeritus Professor of Finance, University of Alabama

Lynn F. Anderson
Assistant Director, Institute of Public Affairs, University of Texas

M. Mason Gaffney
Professor of Economics, University of Wisconsin—Milwaukee

Peter House
University of Wisconsin—Milwaukee

Richard W. Lindholm
Dean, School of Business Administration, University of Oregon

Carl McGuire
Chairman, Department of Economics, University of Colorado

Albert Pleydell
President, Management Services Associates, Inc., and President, Robert Schalkenbach Foundation

William S. Vickrey
Chairman, Department of Economics, Faculty of Political Science, Columbia University

Elsie M. Watters
Director, State-Local Research, Tax Foundation, Inc.

Preface

Both economy and polity have often been influenced by economic and institutional cycles. So also has the property tax. This ancient levy and opinion about its quality have moved through many different phases. The tax base has expanded and contracted. The relative use of the tax has waxed, waned, and waxed again. Its public image, as well as its evaluation by specialists, has varied considerably over time.

The property tax has been roundly condemned from time out of mind. Some experts have predicted that, unless greatly and, indeed, promptly improved, this fiscal institution is destined for early oblivion. Others—apparently thinking the existing pattern unresponsive to changing circumstances—anticipate no significant change in present property tax arrangements. Despite such conflicting judgments, it is not unreasonable to expect that some form of the property tax will remain as an important fiscal arrangement for the foreseeable future. Accordingly, questions both about barriers to change and about improvement possibilities are of continuing significance.

This book contains the papers presented and the summarized discussion recorded at a conference on the property tax and its administration conducted by the Committee on Taxation, Resources, and Economic Development (TRED), an association of academic economists concerned with natural resource taxation. The conference was held at Kenwood Hall, the continuing education center of the University of Wisconsin—Milwaukee, from July 6 through July 8, 1967. The participants considered whether and to what extent administrative patterns and problems, including the assessment process, are obstacles to change in property tax arrangements and to possible use of land value taxation. The twelve papers here recorded include treatment of this topic, ranging from direct to rather oblique analysis. Taken together they illuminate the conference subject and suggest an emergent consensus. To this reader, the conference record leads to the conclusion that, while the administrative record of the property tax ranges from the simply undistinguished to the clearly incredible, its best performance demonstrates that effective, even-handed administration is quite possible. In addition, predictable future administrative developments, including improved application of data processing to the assessment of property for *ad valorem* tax purposes as well as to the general administration of the tax, will increase the capacity of property tax managers to provide effective, equitable, efficient, and economical administration. Accordingly, property tax administration need not be a bar to the creative redesign of the property tax. That can come about when and if it appears desirable on policy or equity grounds to property tax policy makers who propose tax change and to the electorate who must ultimately decide the quality and character of the tax systems through which they will provide resources for the public sector and services for themselves.

This volume is in four parts, followed by a concluding discussion of the conference subject by participants and invited discussants. The twelve papers provide a wide-ranging consideration of the elements of property tax administration. They also provide a substantial if incomplete basis for appraisal of property tax policy alternatives.

In Part I Arthur D. Lynn, Jr., considers the socio-economic environment and concludes that, while past property tax administrative patterns have been imperfect, the potential for effective administrative performance exists and in fact is far greater now than in the past. Harold Groves takes a long view of the administrability of the property tax and finds evidence for ending his paper on an optimistic note.

Part II covers the adminstrative organization of the property tax. Kenneth C. Back examines the need for improved administration and notes that, while this tax has had a singularly high resistance to change in the past, the current is now running strongly in favor of upgrading the organizational base of property tax administration. John D. Cole II describes the contribution of electronic data processing to property tax administration and concludes that it will provide major assistance in handling the considerable input data required for effective property tax appraisals. Ronald B. Welch also considers this subject in Part IV and, on the basis of the California experience, suggests that the improvements in both assessment and equalization made possible by the computer are of a high order of significance. Paul V. Corusy indicates the congeries of property tax problems that call for legislative action and finds much to be done.

Part III centers on the assessment process. Daniel M. Holland and William M. Vaughn consider self-assessment within a context of benefits and penalties as a substitute for, or an adjunct to, administrative assessment systems. Self-assessment, appropriately constrained, is considered a useful method, pending effective implementation of perhaps more sophisticated arrangements. Anthony G. Ferraro treats the techniques and difficulties of assessing minerals in place, other natural resources, and agricultural realty. His paper notes that not all property tax problems can be solved by improved administration alone and indicates the importance of periodic modernization of legal assessment standards as well as of the climate within which the tax administrator works.

Part III concludes with three papers dealing with assessment standards and the response of the assessment process to change. Frederick D. Stocker considers the administrative and equity problems generated by property tax assessment of undeveloped land in urban-fringe areas and suggests relief by means of limited tax deferrals. Henry Aaron reviews the merits of full value assessment and scientific and economical methods for achieving this objective. A. M. Woodruff presents an appraisal of assessment standards with an aside about property tax patterns in Taiwan.

Part IV centers on the relation of administration and the evolving content and character of property tax policy. Shelley

M. Mark describes Hawaii's Land Use Law, a measure designed to control land use so as to maintain environmental quality under conditions of rapid economic development, against the backdrop of Hawaii's centralized tax system. This paper concludes that, although final judgment would be premature, such legislation provides a basis for greater consistency and uniformity in assessment practices as well as an arrangement for systematic land use planning. In the final paper in Part IV, Ronald B. Welch, the always-stimulating dean of property tax administrators, looks ahead and sees a continued improvement in property tax administration. Wider use of state determinations of average assessment levels and more sophisticated use of sales data by assessing agencies are expected. Such uses derive from effective application of third generation computers to the appraisal process.

During the discussion session that terminated the conference, it was suggested that marked improvement of property tax administration is an available option in present-day tax systems. Similarly, despite present defects, potential administrative capacities are of such a quality that future property tax design decisions may be made largely on the basis of other determinative factors. This conclusion, while limited in scope, will be encouraging to those concerned with rationality in taxation. It has not always been so.

The conference and this book derive from the continuing program of the Committee on Taxation, Resources, and Economic Development; the help of the several members of that committee contributed largely to this undertaking. The continuing support of the Robert Schalkenbach Foundation, its president, Albert Pleydell, and its executive secretary, Miss V. G. Peterson, is gratefully acknowledged. The effective cooperation and stimulating inputs of all participants of the conference made it a pleasant, worthwhile, and instructive experience. In addition, the assistance and forbearance of the several institutions with which conference members are associated merit acknowledgment. In this connection, it is by no means inappropriate to record that The Ohio State University was helpful and that my secretary, Marlyn Wyman, was invaluable.

Finally, I thank Weld S. Carter, who induced my participation in this project and then served as an effective partner and good friend during its implementation.

ARTHUR D. LYNN, JR.

Columbus, Ohio
April, 1968

Contents

List of Tables and Figures

Tables

Figures

I. AN OVERVIEW

𝕀𝕀 *Arthur D. Lynn, Jr.*

The Institutional Context of Property Tax Administration

Environmental Constraints

At the 1965 Conference of the Committee on Taxation, Resources, and Economic Development my paper concluded that, "Property taxation has developed out of an essentially agrarian background and, despite the efforts of many over a rather extended period, it is not yet well adjusted to an essentially urban society. This challenge remains, not only for the scholar and the lawmaker, but for all society."[1]

The passage of two years—an instant in the continuum of history—has provided no basis for a change in this opinion. Accordingly, a conference devoted to the property tax and its administration needs to consider the institutional context which simultaneously limits and supports potentials for improved *ad valorem* property tax administration. The environment of the tax, the tax itself, and the complex continuing interaction between the two are briefly analyzed here.

This examination may or may not fall within the sphere of economics;[2] doubtless, many would leave this sort of thing to the sociologist, the historian, and the anthropologist, or perhaps to that recent discoverer of technostructure, John Kenneth Galbraith.[3] Whatever the correct disciplinary classification may be, the big and disturbing questions dealing with the institutional environment and its evolving interactive relation with economic and administrative behavior require analysis. While analytical rigor may be elusive in this area, there is little doubt about the relevance of asking again why the property tax has evolved at only a glacial rate.

As Dick Netzer has so well said,

> The conventional wisdom, perhaps, is that the property tax is inherently a sound tax, properly utilized as the number one revenue source for non-federal government, but that it is all too often administered badly. My view is that the quality of administration of the property tax is *universally* worse than the quality of administration we have come to expect in connection with income and sales taxes. (The measure of quality here is the extent to which similarly situated taxpayers—as defined by the tax laws—actually do pay identical taxes.) In some jurisdictions, the quality of property tax administration is only moderately worse than the quality of good nonproperty tax administration; in others, it is abysmally worse. But nowhere does it really match nonproperty tax administration.[4]

Harold Groves has succinctly summarized the matter with the comment, "We are making progress but not enough."[5] In another connection, Groves has likened property tax reform reports to repetitive sermons from the same pulpit but has noted their continued relevance because of inaction by decision-makers.[6]

If we accept the Netzer-Groves assessment as correct, the question arises as to why we do not apply the already known, the recently rediscovered, and the presently perceived to this venerable fiscal institution instead of merely discussing the problem once more as if it were the weather. Since we seldom do so, one may still inquire: How does the institutional environment affect this particular facet of contemporary society? Will conflicting tendencies toward coherence and disturbance run together in a neutralizing counterpoint which will continue to inhibit effective redesign of property tax administration?

Contemporary Prophets—Views from Olympus

All societies have included specialists in forecasting the future as well as those appraising the near-term present. While their methodology has shown a remarkable variety over time, practitioners of the long view are apparently an inevitable and, indeed, a desired presence. The division of labor they represent accords with the insights of Smithian economics and with the perennial desire of mankind for certainty where very little actually exists. Short-term economic forecasting is hard enough; appraisal of the grand sweep and direction of institutional development is considerably more difficult. Yet, fortunately, just as there are those who will ride at any fence, there are those who seek to appraise long-term trends and illuminate the policy alternatives they suggest.[7] A complete review of the literature is clearly beyond the scope of this paper. However, selective sampling provides a foundation for consideration of the interwoven relations of the socio-economic environment and property tax administrative potentials. Let us then use A. A. Berle, John W. Gardner, and Robert L. Heilbroner as examples of those who, at least on occasion, consider the character of the present and the probable quality of the future environment.

Berle, discussing property, production, and revolution, observes:

> Though its outline is still obscure, the central mass of the twentieth century American economic revolution has become discernible. Its driving forces are five: (1) immense increase in productivity; (2) massive collectivization of property devoted to production, with accompanying decline of individual decision-making and control; (3) massive dissociation of wealth from active management; (4) growing pressure for greater distribution of such passive wealth; (5) assertion of the individual's right to live and consume as the individual chooses.[8]

Berle sees an emergent society with the property institution greatly changed and the economic problem either solved or capable of solution.[9] However, he recognizes that there is plenty to be done before the millennium arrives.

John W. Gardner has recently compiled a list of challenges facing this society, introducing it with the comment that, "Anyone giving thought to the tasks facing science and technology may find it useful to have in mind the problems our society faces in the years immediately ahead. Thoughtful people with time on their hands can make up their own lists; for those without time, here's mine . . . ."[10] Regardless of time availability, Gardner's list provides a useful and perceptive statement of the problems confronting our polity; he includes those related to (1) building an enduring peace, (2) inducing economic development, (3) effecting population control, (4) providing equal opportunity, (5) creating an effective educational system, (6) bringing new life to cities, (7) maintaining environmental quality, (8) reshaping government, (9) stimulating economic growth, and (10) rebuilding the relationship of the individual to society. After reviewing these by no means insignificant concerns, Gardner then concludes in part:

> Our capacity to create new problems as rapidly as we solve the old has implications for the kind of society we shall have to design. We shall need a society that is sufficiently honest and open-minded to recognize its problems, sufficiently creative to conceive new solutions, and sufficiently purposeful to put these solutions into effect. It should be, in short, a self-renewing society, ready to improvise solutions to problems it won't recognize until tomorrow. The vitality of our science and technology will have a great deal to do with whether we achieve that kind of society.[11]

This apt expression of the major problems of our present environment reminds us that the problem of dealing with them remains. As John Gardner has said elsewhere, "This will strike some as a burdensome responsibility, but it will summon others to greatness."[12]

Several years ago, Robert L. Heilbroner wrote a short piece, "On the Seriousness of the Future," suggesting that our view of the future is often a trivial pep-talk or a traditional and naively optimistic assumption that solutions to problems will in due course be forthcoming.[13] He contends that a frank admission that some problems may be beyond our capacity to solve would be healthy. His essay then draws an acerbic contrast between the "Great Awakening" in the underdeveloped areas of the world and our apparent domestic incapacity to deal effectively with the problems at home which stem from science, size, population growth, complex interdependence, and a far less than totally effective educational system. Heilbroner aptly labels this condition a "Great Paralysis." "What is needed," he argues, "is a fundamental change, both of institutions and of outlook, a new balance between private prerogative and public right: in short, a reformation of that social and economic order we call American capitalism."[14] Then comes the query: "Can a society that half-educates and constantly diverts its citizens, that extols nearly all private and denigrates nearly all public activity, that addresses itself to the problems of the future in the language of the past—can such a society find an adequate response to the challenge of the Great Awakening or to that of the Great Paralysis? I find it hard to answer the question affirmatively."[15]

These several views of our current and prospective environment provide a backdrop for consideration of property tax potentials. They portray a society faced with a substantial number of both internal and external difficulties that claim a first lien on energies, ideas, resources, and innovative capacity. Such a forecast hardly augurs favorably for significant property tax revision; however, judgment is best deferred.

Institutional Counterpoint and Change Potentials

Fiscal institutions change but slowly; major developments require a protracted period for assimilation. So it has been in the past with the property tax. Such fiscal inertia is in part a function of environment. One wonders whether past constraints will continue to retard and restrict otherwise possible future property tax developments.

Ad valorem property taxation developed in a period of both private and public scarcity when agriculture was predominant, transportation and communication primitive, government decentralized, international commitments minimal, and the public sector relatively small. Much of its character and structure was and is the response to that environment. Today conditions are quite different; the context within which tax policy decisions must be made is sharply altered. The current environment is a kaleidoscope considerably modified by the lenses through which one sees it. The following elements in the contemporary American socio-economic environment seem relevant:

1. A great productive capacity and an uneven affluence which raise the hope of banishing scarcity and solving the economic problem while at the same time expanding the aspirations of mankind and thereby creating new congeries of social problems.

2. Variable and not altogether predictable international commitments—military, political, and economic—which limit the distributive reality and the effective economic minima possible in even a mature and affluent economy.

3. Continued urbanization of a scientifically and technologically dominated society, with resultant shifts in the locus of political and economic power.

4. Population growth producing a crowded society at once herd-bound and freedom-seeking.

5. The continued computerization of information handling and the progressive automation of production processes.

6. The expanding demand for and need of new programs provided by the public sector.

7. A continued separation of public sector program expansion requirements—often most acute at the state and local level—and tax levying or resource mobilizing capacity, which is most effective at the national level.

8. An apparent absence of dramatic or sustained major organizational innovation.

The environment suggested by this partial list of relevant factors influences the prospects for property tax modifications, including those designed to improve administration. The interaction of tax pattern and environmental factors conditions the response of this ancient levy to changing circumstances and will determine its future. Interpretation is obviously difficult. It appears probable that more will be asked of the property tax and that, simultaneously, its potential capacity and actual response will tend to diverge. If so, the dichotomy will place even greater burdens and responsibilities upon the property tax administrator. Coupled with this bleak prospect is the encouraging probability that the opportunity for and the means of significantly improved administration will be present. Before a summation, two additional matters merit attention. These are what I will call the standard forecast about property tax change and the changing character of property itself.

The Standard Forecast: Professionalization, Centralization, and Computerization

Business economists concerned with predicting business behavior and the short-term level of economic activity operate at levels ranging from pragmatic simplicity to the distinctly arcane.[16] They often refer to the "standard forecast"—the consensus of observers using conventional techniques. While reliance upon such a norm is not necessarily any wiser than it is daring, reference to the "received wisdom" or the "standard forecast" is by no means inappropriate. In fact, ignoring such evidence when it is available suggests either exaggerated confidence or distinct unwisdom. This is also true with respect to conventional thought about probable change in property tax arrangements.

What will be termed here the standard forecast of desirable change and adjustment in the property tax focuses upon the application of three ideas to the tax: professionalization, centralization, and computerization, hereinafter referred to as "PCC." From time out of mind—to use that apt phrase of the common law counselor—professionalization of property tax administration, especially of the assessment process, has been suggested by academician and administrator alike. Similarly, frequent recommendation has been made for the centralization of property tax administration, in whole or in part, at the state level or at least closer to the state level.[17] More recently, the utilization of modern data processing capabilities to achieve prompt, effective, and even-handed property tax administration has been repeatedly advised. Proposals within these three "PCC" areas have definite merit and are explored by other papers in this symposium.

Property: New Realities and Conceptual Rigidity

One additional element in the environment of the property tax requires comment—the changing character of property. Property rules are located in the older part of the house of the law. Therein, the legal mind considers property as a creature of the law, as a divisible bundle of rights, as *in rem* or *in personam,* and, within this context, judges accordingly as custom, precedent, ancient wisdom, or current necessity and the right may require. The law retains the familiar and understandable rules that come down to us from an earlier and simpler time, such as the maxim *sic utere tuo ut alienum non laedas* (so use your property as not to injure that of another), while it assimilates the recent and considerably more difficult rules that result from developed urbanism.

Meanwhile, with increased urban, political, and economic complexity, it is not altogether surprising that property concepts are extended to cover, in one way or another, new interests and new relationships.[18] Today much wealth takes the form of rights, relationships, or status rather than of tangible property, be it real or personal. We have moved from status to contract and back again. Regardless of descriptive tags, change and development have come and the one-time symmetry of property rules is substantially eroded.[19] These developments are of great interest and not inconsiderable concern to those analyzing the theory of property, the response of legal norms, and the direction of institutional evolution. It is not apparent that the implications of these matters for property taxation have received similar attention. Little notice is paid by lawyer, tax administrator, or fiscal analyst to the changing nature and scope of property or to the development of new property forms, or, for that matter, to changes in the relative importance of various categories of property, new and old.

Interestingly enough, as property interests have become more complex and diverse, the *ad valorem* tax base has contracted rather than expanded. In a culture that hardly can be said to underemphasize either the automobile or the television receiver, these items of property are often in law or in fact exempt from *ad valorem* taxation. In an economy that has expanded the scope of intangible personal property considerably beyond the imaginations of either the Founding Fathers or the eighteenth-century bar, such property is increasingly untaxed. In one of the most opulent economies in human history, business inventories are often exempt from property taxation. Of course, a good case can be and has been made for most exemption categories. However, the scope of the property tax has simply not kept up with the expanding potential tax base. Proponents of land value taxation may favor this result. However, there is no particularly intimate relationship between the case for land value taxation and the relative contraction of the *ad valorem* tax base. Given the canon of fiscal neutrality and an effective tax administration, one can argue that a broad-based low-rate property tax which included a wide spectrum of taxable property would have merit on both equity and revenue grounds, especially if appropriately coordinated with existing income taxes. However, neither actual tax policy nor positive environmental influences seem to favor this tax design.

An Assessment of Environmental Effects: A Preliminary Opinion

" 'Would you tell me, please, which way I ought to go from here?' (Alice went on.)

" 'That depends a good deal on where you want to get to,' said the Cat."

It is time to pull this tangled skein of disparate ideas together and make a tentative judgment about the effect of the socio-economic environment upon property tax administrative potentials. Caution is required even if one is unconvinced that by 1976 the property tax "will . . . have become an all-but-forgotten relic of an earlier fiscal age."[20]

Rehearsing the obvious and reviewing the probable are not without value. It is reasonable to assume that our society will continue to have enough problems to keep its energies and its effective capacities fully engaged. Whether we like it or not, the patterns of solution to many of these problems are likely to emerge, if at all, at the national or international level. In the near-term future, energy and resources (as distinguished from remedial programs designed to solve or ameliorate urban stress) may well not flow into local government in greater relative amounts than at present. Despite the attractiveness of creative federalism, resource availability, program design, and problem solution are likely to remain predominantly at the federal level.

This conclusion does not imply any reduction in the demands upon and the resource needs of local government. That is, with the tendency for old problems to become more acute and with the ability of our society to generate new needs, even the typical upward mobility of problems in the American federalism will not relieve local governments and the states from the fiscal strains that result from program intensification and expansion. Such is the prospect ahead.

If so, increased reliance upon federal grants, contracts, and aids as well as expanded user charges and nonproperty taxes appears unlikely to reduce materially the continuing pressure for increased property tax revenue productivity and administrative improvement. According to the trends in our present environment, achieving the goals set forth in the standard forecast described earlier may be all that can be reasonably expected for the property tax. Moderate optimism suggests that some professionalization, only limited centralization, and rather significant computerization of property tax administration are the probable line of administrative development. Computerization may induce additional professionalization and administrative centralization; it has done so in other managerial areas.

Nevertheless, the potential for effective property tax administration—if both brains and resources are concentrated—is now far greater than in any previous time. While the institutional environment appears only partially supportive, significant administrative improvement potential exists. Whether or not the purposive will that converts otherwise unrealized potential into effective performance exists in adequate degree remains an open question.

Acknowledgments

The author wishes to express his appreciation for helpful comments and suggestions from Diran Bodenhorn, Paul G. Craig, Kermit Cudd, James Heck, Kenneth Krouse, Pamela and Pauline Lynn, Meno Lovenstein, Clinton Oster, Leo Raskind, Ivan Rutledge, Frederick Stocker, and Marlyn Wyman. They, of course, bear no responsibility for the result. In addition, the author wishes to thank the Office of Academic Affairs of The Ohio State University for financial support toward the preparation of this paper and his colleagues, Novice G. Fawcett and John E. Corbally, Jr., for their kind forbearance during its development.

Notes

1 Arthur D. Lynn, Jr., "Property Tax Developments: Selected Historical Perspectives," in *Property Taxation, USA,* ed. Richard W. Lindholm (Madison: University of Wisconsin Press, 1967), p. 17.

2 See R. A. Gordon, "Institutional Elements in Contemporary Economics," in *Institutional Economics, Veblen, Commons and Mitchell Reconsidered* (Berkeley: University of California Press, 1963), pp. 121–47. Note especially p. 137.

3 John Kenneth Galbraith, *The New Industrial State* (Boston: Houghton Mifflin Company, 1967). Also see Leo J. Raskind, "Professor Galbraith, The Antitrust Laws and Corporate Size," *Utah Law Review,* 1967, pp. 622–32; and Walter Adams, "A Blueprint for Technocracy," *Science,* 157, 532.

4 Dick Netzer, "Some Alternatives in Property Tax Reform," *Tax Policy,* 33, No. 12 (December, 1966), 12.

5 Harold Groves, "Property Tax—Effects and Limitations," *ibid.,* p. 12.

6 *Proceedings of the National Tax Association,* 1964 (Harrisburg: National Tax Association, 1965), p. 156.

7 See, for example, Herman Kahn and Anthony J. Wiener, *The Year 2000* (New York: Macmillan, 1967).

8 A. A. Berle, "Property, Production and Revolution," *Columbia Law Review,* January, 1965, pp. 1–20.

9 On possible effects of solving the economic problem, see J. M. Keynes, "Economic Possibilities for Our Grandchildren (1930)," in *Essays in Persuasion* (New York: W. W. Norton & Co., 1963

reprint), p. 358; and Sebastian de Grazia, *Of Time, Work and Leisure* (New York: Twentieth Century Fund, 1962).

10 John W. Gardner, "The Ten Commitments," *Saturday Review,* July 1, 1967, pp. 39–40.

11 *Ibid.*

12 John W. Gardner, *Self-Renewal: The Individual and the Innovative Society* (New York: Harper & Row, 1963), p. 127.

13 Robert L. Heilbroner, "On the Seriousness of the Future," *The American Scholar,* August, 1963, pp. 556–62.

14 *Ibid.,* p. 561.

15 *Ibid.,* p. 562. See also Robert L. Heilbroner, *The Limits of American Capitalism* (New York: Harper & Row, 1966).

16 See, for example, *How Business Economists Forecast,* ed. William F. Butler and Robert A. Kavesk (Englewood Cliffs, N.J.: Prentice-Hall, 1966).

17 See, for example, Advisory Commission on Intergovernmental Relations, *The Role of the States in Strengthening the Property Tax,* Vol. I (Washington, 1963).

18 See, for example, Charles A. Reich, "The New Property," *Yale Law Journal,* 73 (April, 1964) 733–87.

19 For another view see Daniel Bell, "Notes on the Post-Industrial Society (II)," *The Public Interest,* No. 7, Spring 1967, pp. 102–18.

20 George W. Mitchell, "Is This Where We Came In?" *Proceedings of the National Tax Association,* 1956, p. 494.

Harold M. Groves

Is the Property Tax Conceptually and Practically Administrable?

The Concept of Value

The property tax is said to be a difficult tax to administer because it is based on valuation. Any fool can count the number of sheep going over a fence before he goes to sleep; but it takes a wide-awake expert to evaluate the flock, and two experts might differ in considerable degree on a figure.

Some rhymester has described the role of the property tax assessor as follows:

> To find a value good and true
> Here are three things for you to do
> Consider your replacement cost
> Determine value that is lost
> Analyze your sales to see
> What market value really should be
> Now if these suggestions are not clear
> Copy the figures you used last year.

Of all these suggestions, only the final and contingent one is easy—a fact which accounts perhaps for the report that the sin of plagiarism originated in an assessor's office.

Part of the trouble stems from the fact that value is a subtle and elusive concept. In its broadest sense, valuation is the goal of all our quest for knowledge and wisdom. Subjective conclusions in this endeavor are often described as value judgments. Economic value, one species of this larger genus, is presumably quantifiable and hopefully objective. Still it is often remarked that all value is somebody's estimate;[1] also that valuation is an art rather than or perhaps in addition to a science.

Most commonly, economists define the value of a good as its power in exchange, and this definition—the market value rule —has been adopted by most property tax statutes. But of course this does not mean that, if the assessor places a $10,000 figure on a house and the house is sold next week for $15,000, then the assessor has undervalued this house by one-third. Sales determine value but a particular sale is not conclusive and might be badly off target. Exchanges are made by fools like you and me; why should we assume that the exchangers are better judges of the market than the assessor? Of course an estimate backed by cash is entitled to respect in terms of sincerity, but it is likely to be amateurish compared with the assessor's figure.

If we had fifty identical properties in a community and they all sold simultaneously, one could approximate an objective valuation by calculating an average sales price. One could then claim that he had found an absolute truth among values, a *fact* about which reasonable men could have no difference of opinion. It would be the sort of fact which an opinion poll reveals. But an assessor does not have so simplified a situation in which to work. Probably all his properties differ in some—often many—respects. An adequate data card for a single-family home may provide information concerning more than 100 variables. To be sure, the market does yield evidence concerning these parts of properties in many combinations. If we knew the value of the components and had them all represented, we could plug them into a computer and get the right answer. Thus it is mainly because our analysis and evidence are incomplete that there is a subjective element in assessment. Nevertheless it must appear to many an assessor that he is shooting at a mark which sways with the wind.

Elementary economics often draws a distinction between current market value and normal value, the latter allowing time for long adjustments that smooth out temporary aberrations in the market. Some assessment statutes also make the distinction, calling for valuations at the level for which property would sell *ordinarily*. On one interpretation, at least, this might indicate that at times even a well-established market is not reliable. There might be such a circumstance as all real estate in town selling above or below its "true" value. Fortunately, no doubt, most of the assessors most of the time have conceived no obligation to assume the role of economic forecaster.

But of course there is an inescapable element of futurity in value. One buys with property an expected stream of income stretching on into the indefinite future. The clearest case in which the assessor is tempted to—maybe required to—gamble is that of the rural-urban fringe. Here there may be some relevant sales, but generally the market is so dynamic and imperfect that comparable sales provide no valid basis of assessment. Or take the case of urban land which the assessor is told to value at its most profitable use. Does this include that renewal which will require the cooperation of neighbors or the coercion of government?

Market value, if one could but find it, would probably provide a fair indication of capacity to pay taxes much of the time, but there are notable exceptions. The notorious one is the property built for a highly specialized purpose (New York Stock Exchange) which could not be sold except for a very inferior use. Would it be legitimate to consider the present well-satisfied owner as both buyer and seller? The cases in this category constitute an interesting chapter in our subject, but we shall have to pass over them with the observation that generally—not always—assessors and courts have been able to reason or rationalize their way out of an absurd result.[2]

Question of Administrability

Criticism of the prevailing quality of property tax administration (assessments) has been the feature in public finance literature and in the speeches and reports of officials for at least 100 years.[3] But most of it, especially the recent comment, has laid the blame upon imperfections of practices, procedures, and organization. There has not been much doubt that we could administer the property tax if we would.[4] The Advisory Commission on Intergovernmental Fiscal Relations, in its memorable survey of property tax administration, expressed the view that the assessment performance in a considerable portion of jurisdictions in the United States—mostly large urban districts—is of acceptable quality. To support this view, census surveys of assessment ratios for single-family nonfarm residences are cited. In 1957, the census found 21 percent of the jurisdictions covered had coefficients of dispersion of less than 20 percent; by 1962, the number had risen to 31 percent of the districts.[5]

It remained for Dick Netzer, in his extremely interesting recent book on the general property tax, to raise a profound doubt that the property tax is conceptually and practically administrable with a fair degree of precision and at reasonable cost.[6] He considers a 20-percent margin of error, as cited in the census data above, a low standard of excellence even if most districts were meeting it. If we discovered such loose performance associated with the administration of the sales tax or income tax we would consider it shocking. Netzer notes that the test of property tax in the census was in the category for which one might expect the best performance: single-family homes in metropolitan areas, where property is relatively homogeneous and the market is active. It is hard to imagine what the score would be for industrial real estate, public utilities, and some kinds of personal property. The evidence of discrimination among classes of property is also disturbing; apparently this phenomenon is not only quite widespread but also in many cases deliberate and systematic. Finally Netzer raises the issue of costs: tax base and yield in large urban districts will support adequate expertise and specialization in staff within a cost range of 1 to 2 percent of revenue; but would this be true of thinly populated areas even if the county were everywhere accepted as the unit of authority?

We conclude with the observation that Netzer's indictment

is incisive and persuasive; let us postpone our further reaction until we have reviewed some highlights in the history of the general property tax and its administration.

The Property Tax and Economic Development

In a discerning monograph entitled *A General Theory of Tax Structure Change During Economic Development,* Harley Hinrichs argues that there is a standard evolution of tax models, whether the observation be historical or a cross-section comparison of different countries at the same point of time.[7] Early models stress direct taxes on property and land; later the emphasis turns to levies on international trade, then to internal excise taxes, and finally back again to direct taxes, now featuring personal taxes on income and wealth. The factor of administration, says Hinrichs, plays a large part in this pattern. Thus a reformer should not recommend graduated modern net income taxes for a large role in a relatively primitive economy; in practice they would probably turn out to be "neither modern, nor progressive, nor even income taxes."[8]

But the curious point in Hinrichs' analysis is his finding that the evolution starts with a property tax, the very levy we have singled out for its administrative difficulty. Hinrichs' historical facts seem well grounded; we note from the general chronicles of English history that even before the Norman conquest there were such taxes as the Danegeld, at first levied for tribute and later for national revenue.[9] Following the conquest, William the First developed his famous Doomsday Survey, said to be one of the greatest accomplishments of a great king. It was an elaborate assessment of everything in the king's realm, without an equal in the medieval world. The Angevine kings collected the "scutage" or shield-money, practically a land tax and mostly for the commutation of military service. It seems that for several centuries property taxation worked well enough to be retained as almost the whole tax system. As wealth differentiated, particularly in towns, efforts were made, though not very successfully, to broaden the base of property taxes by including "movables."

Now let us shift the scene to present-day South America, where property taxes are generally of very minor importance and where they are recommended by some critics as especially strategic for expansion. This proposal meets the rejoinder that any substantial use of the property tax must wait for an acceptable valuation of property which in turn is a slow, difficult, arduous project. Professor John Strasma proposes to jump this slow schedule by self-assessment reinforced with an authorization to purchase the land at the figure specified. His ingenious variation of an old idea seeks to make such purchase available under certain conditions to private parties.[10] But our present interest is attracted especially to the question: If the tax authorities in Colombia find the property tax so difficult, how did the medievalists in Britain and elsewhere manage to make the property tax a tolerable success? Hinrichs doesn't attempt a full answer, but he does suggest that feudal attitudes and arrangements may have facilitated the administration and collection of the tax. Thus by the seventeenth century both feudalism and respect for the British property tax had largely disappeared. The national tax itself has now been abandoned with minor qualifications, but remnants survive in the income tax; local rates on property are still the major local source. Valuation, even within these restricted uses, has proved troublesome; it has been entrusted to the Inland Revenue Service.

Evolution of the American Tax

The British tax, when first imported by the American colonies, was a largely personal tax measured by property occupied or by such other elements of capacity to pay as polls and "faculty," or by a combination. It was, so to speak, a tax system complete in itself. Gradually and without losing its feature of local administration, the tax in America took on those qualities of uniformity and universality which gave it such notoriety during the later years of the nineteenth century. Earlier personal features were dropped and intangibles (which the British never tried to tax) were added.

It was at this time that dissatisfaction with the property tax and its administration reached its height. Seligman and Adams stressed the fact that the inclusion of intangibles in the property tax base mixed rights in property with the physical property itself to create an impossible mess of erratic double counting.[11] The confusion provided the assessor with a perfect alibi for a sloppy and illegal assessment; were he to comply courageously and faithfully with the statutes, the property tax would be quite intolerable.

It was during these days that the property tax developed some colorful institutions and records that punctuate its ineptitude. One was tax-fixing, an institution which flourished in Chicago.[12] It flourished on the standing threat of full taxation of intangibles, on the division of authority between a board of assessors and another board of review, each with original assessing authority, and on complete secrecy of operations. In this demoralized state of affairs, assessments ranged from 1 percent to well over 100 percent of sales prices.

This was also the heyday of the institution known as tax ferreting. Under this system the reporting of personal property was farmed out to tax inquisitors on a commission contract. Generally they left a trail of bitterness. Farming out tax administration is an ancient expedient; the experience seems to demonstrate that the ethics of tax administration cannot be maintained except by public officials under oath to follow the law.[13]

Dropping Intangibles

These institutions and this period in property tax administration were so bad that most any change must be for the better. There were several changes and very much for the better. The first improvement was the exemption of some property, notably intangibles, most difficult to assess. The attempt to tax intangibles had corrupted the tax system and tarnished its image. Where intangibles were retained on the tax rolls they were generally classified for a special rate of levy, and in a few cases this feature of the tax was entrusted to state administration. The tax system was broadened with supplementary levies on income, sales, inheritances, and capital stock. Some of these taxes, notably the net income tax, provided a source of information concerning some kinds of personal property and thus facilitated property tax administration.

State Assessment in Some Areas

A second improvement transferred from local to state agencies several of the areas of assessment most difficult to manage. The state agency was usually the state tax commission or department, which itself had been an important development. Principal classes of property so transferred in most states were railroads, public utilities, and mines. How well the states have succeeded (or may succeed) in these special areas is a long and complicated chapter which I shall not discuss in any detail. In general, it can be said that the assessment and apportionment of such property is as difficult as any in the property tax field; that adequate performance requires a suitable administrative organization and staff; that, while techniques in the field have been much refined, a considerable subjective element in the performance remains. Finally and in spite of the last observation, we may conclude optimistically that central assessment of railroad and public utility property at its best is probably as good as local assessment of other property also at its best.[14] Sloppy and dishonest work is not hard to find in either area. Quite aside from valuation, mention should be made of the fact that railroads are often, though not universally, victims of discriminatory equalization.[15]

State Supervision and Equalization of Local Assessments

A change regarded by many at the time as an improvement proposed to get the states out of the property tax business. Traditionally they had relied on the general property tax as their major source of revenue and had employed local assessments, with some modifications, as the base for their tax. The state tax was thus a locally collected, centrally shared tax—the reverse of some present-day "piggy-back" systems. However, without thorough-going equalization, the system invited so-called "competitive undervaluation" to reduce the community's share of the state tax. Under this influence, assessments in many localities depreciated like money in a run-away inflation, a blight from which they never fully recovered.

It was, in part, the desire to sidestep this problem that induced some states to abandon the general property tax in favor of their municipalities. But the strategy didn't work. The determination of full value of taxable property by districts still proved necessary for a variety of purposes—among them the equitable application of the state's own assessment of railroads.

Thus state tax agencies began to develop their highly significant role of scientific mass assessment of districts. This took the form of sample studies of local assessments, comparing the samples with sales or independent appraisals. Gradually refinements followed—the "fielding" of sales to rule out biased ones, the supplementation of sales with independent appraisals, and the use of classified samples. Along with this appeared the new institution of *supervision*—a mixed system of local autonomy and central education, persuasion, and assistance. Added too was *reassessment,* generally a vehicle of local correction with state assistance at local request. There is a range of quality in the application of these tools of intergovernmental relations. At their best they seem to have gone a long way in making a silk purse out of a sow's ear.

Professionalization of the Assessor's Office and Practice

It comes as something of a shock to learn that the local assessor in the early days of Wisconsin was not an appraiser at all; he was a "collector of lists and administrator of oaths." Property owners were supposed to self-assess their property and take a solemn oath to the list. The Supreme Court held that a sworn list was final except for an action for perjury.[16] The system was castigated by early governors as principally effective in undermining "the solemnity of oaths." In the late 1860's it was largely abandoned in favor of the assessor's own count and appraisal. Along with self-listing went drastic penalties for dishonest reporting. The experience should have established two principles of tax administration: unless reinforced by other evidence, self-reporting will not provide a fair and adequate tax base; threat of drastic penalty of and by itself will not help very much.

The inauguration of a new era in Wisconsin tax experience, with its state tax department and scientific equalization and supervision of assessments, brought some agitation for the abandonment of the local assessment function. In the early years the Wisconsin Tax Commission repeatedly recommended radical changes: state-chosen civil service assessors, county-wide jurisdiction for assessment, and state power to discharge local assessors.[17] In Wisconsin proposals of this kind have met a stone wall of opposition to centralization. Such legislation has fared better in other states—in Iowa, for instance, where, with one stroke of the pen, so to speak, the number of assessors was reduced from 2500 to 120. Only cities with population of 10,000 or more were left with independent assessors of their own.

Nevertheless we have made some progress toward professionalization even in Wisconsin. By legislation enacted soon after World War II (1949), appointment of assessors by qualifying examinations became mandatory in first-class cities, and it is permissive in all cities and villages and in towns of more than 5000 population. There has been a trend toward civil service in very large cities, toward appointment with some regard to merit and tenure in second-class and third-class cities, and for consolidation of offices (to create full-time jobs) in smaller cities. The term of office of elected assessors was increased in 1949 from one to two years. Thus most local people can have professionalized service in the assessor's office if they want it.

Notwithstanding the above, a very considerable part of local assessment in Wisconsin is done by what the critics would label "amateurs." The critics properly add that imperfections at the local level cannot be offset by superimposing a hierarchy of regulatory agencies and functions to correct original mistakes. Moreover, a 25 percent turnover of assessors at each election is obviously wasteful. In small cities and villages the local assessor is likely to be a janitor, plumber, printer, or grocer. Wisconsin's good reputation in property tax administration exists in spite of these features and not because of them. But it does support the conclusion that excellence in intergovernmental relations may be at least as important as professionalization at the local level.[18]

Conclusion: Is the Property Tax Administrable?

Let us return to the question which we posed in our title and which we left dangling in the midst of Netzer's skepticisms. We conclude that Netzer is overly pessimistic. In criticizing the selection of 20 percent as a standard of excellence in coefficients of dispersion, he forgets that both the standard and the performance in general property tax work are subject to some error. To judge an assessor strictly on the conformity of his work to particular sales is to judge him in a court of his inferiors. Some studies by Warner Doering, Wisconsin's state property tax chief, indicate that coefficients of dispersion based upon sales exaggerate an assessor's inaccuracies by 50 percent or more.[19]

"Rough justice" of taxation, it seems, is tolerably satisfied within the range of error and uncertainty that we are considering. Compared with other uncertainties—incidence of sales taxes, for instance—the imprecision is well short of scandalous; the income tax, when it involves depreciation, also depends on judgment.

As for Netzer's skepticism concerning costs in rural county districts, he assumes that all skills will be necessary in all districts. Where a workload is insufficient to support a needed skill, the latter could be supplied by the state office.[20]

Finally the trend of recent history gives some warrant for optimism. If we make as much progress improving property tax administration in the next sixty-five years as we did in the last, we could be well along the road toward acceptable standards of excellence.

Notes

1 See, for instance, the observations in "Report of the Committee on Model Property Tax Assessment and Equalization Methods"

(Arthur D. Lynn, Jr., Chairman), *Proceedings of the National Tax Association Conference*, 1964, p. 181: "Market value lies in the field of opinion—the opinion of the owner, appraiser, realtor, mortgagee and assessor." Or the same report, p. 176, quoting C. M. Chapman: "In the assessment field, whether it be general property or utility property, no state, so far as we know, wishes to deny the assessing official the element of judgment in his final determination. Of course judgment, to be really worth the name, must be informed, otherwise it is nothing more than a guess."

2 The problem is discussed by James C. Bonbright, *Valuation of Property* (New York: McGraw-Hill, 1937), I, 472–79.

3 As far back as 1841, Territorial Governor Doty of Wisconsin observed: "The system of taxation throughout the territory is considered as unequal, illegal and highly oppressive." Message of Governor James D. Doty, 1841, in *Territory of Wisconsin Documents*, 1837–42 (Madison); R. V. Phelan, *The Financial History of Wisconsin*, Bulletin of the University of Wisconsin, Economics and Political Science Series (Madison, 1908), Vol. 2.

4 Witness the confidence of the Advisory Commission on Intergovernmental Relations, *The Role of the States in Strengthening the Property Tax* (Washington, D.C., 1963), p. 33: "The mythology of unfeasibility stems from trying to administer a highly complex tax system by methods that were barely adequate for the simple types of taxable property in the early days of the Republic."

5 For discussion see Dick Netzer, *Economics of the Property Tax* (Washington, D.C.: The Brookings Institution, 1966), pp. 177–82. However, as we shall see, Netzer gets little comfort from the census evidence.

6 *Ibid.*, pp. 173–83.

7 Harley Hinrichs, *A General Theory of Tax Structure* (Cambridge, Mass.: Law School of Harvard University, 1966).

8 *Ibid.*, p. 11.

9 Some historians claim that the Danegeld levies were very severe, amounting perhaps to a third of the produce of the land. These levies are said to have been responsible for considerable "feudalization" of a once-free peasantry.

10 John Strasma, *Market-Enforced Self-Assessment for Real Estate Taxes* (Madison: Land Tenure Center, University of Wisconsin, 1965).

11 Edwin R. A. Seligman, *Essays in Taxation*, 10th ed. (New York: Macmillan, 1925), Ch. 2; Henry Carter Adams, *The Science of*

Finance (New York: Henry Holt and Co., 1898), pp. 361–74. There is an important class of intangibles, such as business good will, which involves no duplication, but this was more often than not ignored by the law.

12 Described in Herbert Simpson's *Tax Racket and Tax Reform in Chicago* (Chicago: Institute for Economic Research, Northwestern University, 1930).

13 John E. Brindley, *History of Taxation in Iowa* (Iowa City: State Historical Society, 1911), I, 310–56. Before 1900, tax ferreting had been used by some counties and it received support by the Iowa Court where a fee of 50 percent of collected taxes was involved (*Shinn* v. *Cunningham,* 120 Iowa 383, 1903). The law of 1900 sanctioned tax ferrets but limited their fee to 15 percent of collections resulting from their efforts (*Acts of Iowa,* 1900, Ch. 50). Some tax ferrets who came from outside the state operated sporadically, skimmed the cream in a given territory, and made little attempt to cover a field with thoroughness and impartiality. Others differed from those just described only in that they were local people. In ten or fifteen counties, the tax ferrets covered the ground consistently, thoroughly, and impartially. It was claimed in legislative debates that the tax ferrets served principally to mulct the widows and orphans, but this was denied by the Tax Ferrets Association and evidence seems to bear out the latter's contention. Brindley expressed the opinion that tax ferrets should be retained until some more advantageous positive substitute could be offered to supplant them.

14 Advisory Commission on Intergovernmental Relations, *The Role of the States in Strengthening the Property Tax,* Vol. 1, Ch. 13.

15 *Ibid.,* pp. 168–79.

16 *Matheson* v. *Town of Mazomanie,* 20 Wisconsin 191 (1865).

17 *Reports of the Wisconsin Tax Commission,* 1916–24, especially 1918, pp. 13–20.

18 See Clara Penniman, "Property Tax Equalization in Wisconsin," *National Tax Journal,* June, 1961, pp. 187–89. Logically the good intergovernmental relations might be extended to provide local voters and officials with the means to judge for themselves whether the assessor is doing his job satisfactorily. In its equalization and sales-ratio studies, the Wisconsin Tax Department in effect makes an audit of local assessment work. Why shouldn't the facts on dispersion of assessments among classes and items of property be published for local consideration?

Where there is *de jure* local responsibility, there should be such in fact and it should be concentrated in one agency. Too often in many systems, assessment and review agencies divide and confuse responsibility.

19 Warner W. Doering, "The Use of Statistical Techniques in Equity Determinations," *Proceedings of the National Tax Association Conference,* 1964, pp. 390–400.

20 Incidentally, it should be noted that one way to minimize the concern about poor property tax administration is to make the tax itself less important. In this direction, one sees merit in the Heller-Pechman plan for federal tax sharing, which, however, is the subject for a paper by itself and a long one.

II. ADMINISTRATIVE ORGANIZATION

Kenneth Back

Potential for
Organizational Improvement of
Property Tax Administration

Property taxation in America has varied both with the climate of public opinion and with the level of economic development but on the whole has tended to resist change. There is every indication, however, that it will adjust more rapidly to the demands of today and tomorrow. The striking changes during the past twenty-five or thirty years alone and the accelerated pace with which they have been occurring would seem to indicate that this ancient tax has entered a truly revolutionary era. The changes are taking place on a number of fronts. Once-complacent taxpayers are demanding better equalization with ever-louder voices as property tax burdens continue to rise. The courts are handing down precedent-setting assessment decisions. The states, which had virtually withdrawn from the property tax field when state property tax levies were largely replaced by sales and income taxes during the Depression days, have renewed their interest in property tax administration and are giving increasing amounts of assistance to local assessment districts. Significant developments also are occurring within the assessing profession itself. Assessors through their own efforts are making great strides in increasing their knowledge and competence and in becoming more professionalized.

While achieving the goals of equitable assessment and efficient administration have long perplexed economists, tax administrators, and others, there is a growing consensus that no real improvement in the quality of assessments can be made without first improving its administration. Proper administration is a crucial factor in the operation of any tax and especially the property tax, which on all counts is by far the most difficult of all taxes to administer. Good administration can often make a poor tax tolerable, whereas poor administration will nearly always make an otherwise good tax intolerable.

The essence of most of the criticism leveled at the property tax is that it is not properly administered, and there are those who question whether it can be fairly and effectively administered. Fortunately, there are developing a widespread interest in property taxation and a recognition of the fact that its administration can and must be improved regardless of any feelings concerning its inherent qualities as a tax compared to other forms of taxation. Since administration cannot function properly without good organization, there is a great need and potential for organizational improvements. The successful administration of any program or function requires the application of proper administrative techniques by capable personnel operating within the framework of a sound organization.

In an earlier era, the assessing job consisted of little more than recording the owner's estimate of value or copying the roll from year to year. This required very little in the way of organization or assessment know-how. Considerably more is being demanded today by the courts, the taxpayers, and the assessors themselves. The taxpayers and the courts are demanding equitable assessments, and more and more assessors are beginning to realize that their job requires the full-time attention and skills of a competent, well-trained professional equipped with all the modern-day tools available, including organizational advances. A workable distribution of powers and duties among assessing agencies and among the personnel within each such agency is of fundamental importance to successful administration of the property tax. While many experts have expounded upon various solutions to improving property tax administration—and, incidentally, there appears to be no shortage of experts in the property tax—the four key areas which appear to hold the most promise are (1) a workable law that lends itself to good administration, (2) assessment districts large enough to support a professional staff with a well-structured internal organization, (3) competent assessment personnel with adequate pay and tenure of office, and (4) adequate financial support. It is readily apparent that few, if any, jurisdictions measure up to all four of these criteria.

One of the major deterrents to effective assessment administration in the United States is the extreme geographical fragmentation of this function and, in some cases, the existence of overlapping assessment districts, which has caused problems of coordination, increased the cost of assessing, and created inequities. The property tax, as the primary source of local tax revenues, traditionally has been administered by the political subdivision it financed. Responsibility for assessment administration is divided among some 15,000 separate local tax districts that operate virtually autonomously with a minimum of review and supervision. This geographical fragmentation of the assessment function results in many assessing offices which are too small to realize the economies of larger scale operations and often cannot even support a single full-time assessor. Efficient administration is impossible under these conditions. In more recent years, the states have been moving in the direction of county assessment units to eliminate districts too small to support adequately a professional assessment job. Much more needs to be done, however, especially in the urban areas where the need for revenues is greatest.

A type of consolidation which has been tried in recent years is the metropolitan area assessment district. One such experiment which has been quite successful involved the city of Toronto, Canada, and twelve suburban municipalities. The Toronto metropolitan area assessment office was given the sole responsibility for all assessments on which the levies of both the metropolitan area government council and the local councils in the area were based. Nashville, Tennessee, is another example of the benefits to be derived from consolidation. Combining the staffs of both the county and the city assessing offices and utilizing them in reorganized job assignments to reflect the best capabilities of the staff members made it possible for the new metropolitan assessing office to review and equalize assessments to a far greater extent than had been possible before. The consolidation provided a much-needed opportunity to organize the new assessment office into a more effective working unit.

As the experiences of Hawaii and Australia demonstrate, it is also possible to administer the assessment function effectively on the state level. When the areas involved are large, branch offices with some degree of autonomous authority and responsibility can be used. In some states, such as Kentucky and Maryland, the assessment function is a state responsibility even though the original assessment is performed by an elected or appointed county assessor, who is paid and supervised by the state. Transferring assessing, which is a technical professional job, to a higher level of government need not impair local sovereignty. Authority to set rates and control local spending can be retained where it belongs at the local level.

Another factor which has complicated property tax administration is the existence of overlapping assessment districts. Though approximately two-thirds of the states now use the county as the basic assessment unit, overlapping assessment districts still exist in some of these states. These districts were created to serve special local government authorities that had been granted separate taxing powers in part because of a general belief that assessing was a legitimate exercise of home-rule powers and in part because of dissatisfaction with the quality of the existing assessments. In some cases, the assessments were not at a high enough level to provide the newly created authority the necessary revenue or borrowing authority under state rate and debt limitations.

Some states have taken steps to eliminate overlapping assessment districts, which generally have proved annoying to taxpayers, expensive to maintain, and subversive of good assessment administration. A better assessment job can be done at lower cost if the duplication of effort is eliminated by either consolidating the overlapping districts or requiring the overlapping district to use the assessment roll of the primary assessment district.

Regardless of its geographical size, an assessment district requires a proper internal organization to be truly effective. Assessment administration has long suffered from what management analysts call "organization dry-rot." This malady is characterized by resistance to change and a tendency to perform the same functions in exactly the same manner regardless of changing needs. The assessment function has undergone far-reaching changes in recent decades. The assessor today is confronted, on the one hand, by a rapidly changing real estate market and a wide range of property types to be valued and, on the other hand, by taxpayer demands for equalization that grow more intense with each rise in property tax rates. Hence, methods that were acceptable fifty years ago are no longer satisfactory.

The need for more effective organization of the assessment function exists whether a capital or a site value system of property taxation is used. Two recognized American authorities recently studied property taxation in Australia and New Zealand, which use both systems, and concluded that the most valuable lessons to be learned from the experiences of these countries were in the areas of administration and organization.[1] The study revealed that the quality of assessment work by the departments of the valuers general in Australia and New Zealand compares with the best, rather than the average, in the United States. It was felt the high quality of Australian and New Zealand assessments was due largely to consolidation of this function in single departments covering areas large enough to support qualified experts, the professional quality of the personnel, the civil service status of the officials and their independence from political influence, and the multipurpose approach of the centralized valuation departments, their valuation being for practically all public purposes in addition to taxation. As the study indicated, the technical task of assessing remains essentially the same regardless of the tax system used, though the procedures and emphasis given to the available indicators of value vary somewhat.

The degree to which an assessor achieves an equalized assessment roll, the efficiency with which he operates, and the degree of public understanding and approval he attains will depend largely on how well his office is organized and managed. Some clearly defined plan of organization is a necessity, and it should be designed to promote the most efficient performance of the assessment task, considering the nature of the work, the operations required, the time factors, and many other variables. Even the smallest staff can perform more effectively if it is organized properly. Of the five generally recognized basic principles of management—namely, planning, organizing, directing, controlling, and coordinating—none is more important than organizing. It is through organization that the other principles are executed. It is the means of directing, controlling, and carrying out program plans. Lines of responsibility and authority, work specialization, and supervisory channels are all functions of organization.

There are two major types of organization commonly used in assessors' offices: that according to function and that according to geography. In a functional organization, the assessor's staff is divided along the lines of the special types of work carried on. This would mean that all the field work would be handled by appraisal specialists, all the clerical work by others, and someone else would be responsible for exemption decisions and defense of appeals. Further specialization among the appraisal staff might include commercial, residential, and industrial property specialists, land specialists, and building cost estimators. Such a plan permits staff members to become expert in their own speciality and tends to promote equal treatment of all properties in the district. On the other hand, none of the staff members becomes really familiar with the entire assessment process, and, unless an experienced assessor reviews the overall property value, there is a danger that the parts will not add up to the correct total. Moreover, in geographically large districts, a strictly functional plan tends to be cumbersome because of the amount of travel required of each field man.

A geographic organization approach divides the work according to areas of the taxing district. A strict application of this approach would result in the assignment to each section of one or more persons who are responsible for all the assessment work in their area. For example, in his own section each person would make the field inspection, appraise all types of property, do all the clerical work in the office, determine the taxability of each property, and defend appeals. This tends to reduce travel time and expense and acquaints each staff member with the assessment process from beginning to end. Major disadvantages of the geographic approach are the difficulty of finding assessors trained to value all types of properties and the problem of assuring equality of treatment of properties located in different assessment areas. Any variation in assessment standards caused by differences in individual judgment will produce assessment inequalities. In addition, none of the staff members is able to specialize since each must perform such a wide range of duties.

The organization type best suited to any given tax district will depend on the size and characteristics of the district and the requirements of law. Most assessment laws require that land and buildings be valued separately and carried on the rolls as separate entries. This is an archaic requirement that should be abolished. Some degree of functional specialization is desirable but less is possible in smaller offices. The problem of obtaining equal treatment of all properties must be overcome if the geographic approach is to be used, although some geographic division may be desirable when there are many properties to be valued.

Several other guidelines can be cited which will govern the ultimate choice of an organization pattern. Activities should be assigned so as to utilize the skills of the staff most effectively and economically and so as to promote the development of additional desired skills. Hence, clerical and record-keeping tasks should be segregated from those requiring higher levels of professional competence. Too often, appraisers are called on to do clerical work that could be performed more efficiently by the clerical staff. This can be avoided by providing adequate clerical staff to allow appraisers to devote their entire time to the appraisal task. To promote maximum performance, responsibility and authority must be clearly delegated to staff members. No single assessor can successfully manage an organization of any size and perform all the work to be done. The best way to get the job done is to assign tasks to people capable of performing them and give them responsibility and authority for these tasks.

The first step in any reorganization effort is to define the objectives sought and the tasks to be performed. The objective of an assessment program is to produce assessments which are equalized in relation to market value and which accurately and promptly reflect changes in market values. Ideally, this means that every property should be assessed every year at 100 percent of market value. In recognition of this, a number of states legally require that assessments represent full market value, and some also have made annual reassessment mandatory. However, no one to my knowledge has accomplished this ideal since assessment changes must of necessity lag somewhat behind market changes. The goal, nonetheless, should be to come as close as possible with available resources and knowledge.

The assessment function involves the following major types of work:

1. Locate and identify all properties in the assessment district, a task which includes mapping, drafting, numbering of parcels, and formulation of a plan for updating both area and ownership.

2. Establish a convenient system for taking inventory and recording building characteristics and other information concerning each property.

3. Determine the market value of each property on the basis of available value indicators within prescribed time limits.

4. Determine the taxability of each property on the basis of existing tax exemption statutes.

5. Establish programs to determine the degree of uniformity of the assessments.

6. Defend assessments upon appeal.

The only way to carry out an efficient assessment program is to plan carefully every function to be performed. An organization is generally successful to the extent that it plans a program and executes the program as planned. In order to formulate such a plan, the time, space, and personnel requirements of the work must be estimated along with the available resources of money, men, and materials.

Once a plan of action has been made and the total requirements and resources have been determined, organization is simply a matter of dividing the work into individual job specialities at various levels of responsibility and grouping the positions into homogeneous operating units headed by technically skilled supervisors. Some of the general guidelines which should be taken into consideration when these decisions are being made have already been discussed. They include the need to assign personnel to jobs for which they are best suited, the role of specialization, and the requirements for delegating responsibility and authority. As I mentioned earlier, there are a number of ways an assessor can divide the work. The choice regarding the functional or geographic approach will depend on the size and other characteristics of the assessing district. The assessor must decide which organizational pattern will be most effective for him in view of the magnitude of his particular assessing job and the available resources. There is no one pattern which will meet the requirements of all assessing districts.

For example, the organizational problems of a very large assessing jurisdiction such as Los Angeles County, which has 1300 permanent employees and an annual budget of $11,000,000, are very different and far more complex than those of a small district with only one assessor and a clerk. According to James R. Vine, the Chief Deputy Assessor, the Los Angeles County Assessor's Office was reorganized to streamline its operations and improve the quality of the assessment of its 1,800,000 properties.[2] The office is divided into five parts. Three are concerned with general administrative and house-keeping operations and the other two with the functions of appraisal and appraisal standards. A relatively new approach in assessment organization is the Assessment Standards Division which is staffed with senior appraisal personnel and is responsible for planning, programming, and evaluating all appraisal work of the office. The division establishes all appraisal methods and procedures and annually determines those properties to be revalued by comparing assessed values with sales and selected appraisals. The appraisal staff values those properties selected for reappraisal by the assessments standards staff.

An equally important phase of planning the organization of an assessment program is the establishment and maintenance of controls on both the quantity and the quality of production. There should be a system of reporting to advise management of the completion of plans as scheduled. These reports also should inform management of inadequacies in performance or failures to meet schedules so that plans and schedules can be revised to improve the operation and performance of tasks.

Another requisite to an effective assessment program is experienced personnel who know how to analyze property value information and apply it to arrive at equalized assessed values. In view of the growing mood of protest of the taxpayers, whose tax bite has been getting larger and larger, it does not make any sense to leave property tax administration in the hands of amateurs, even if honest and well-meaning. It has become increasingly apparent that one basic essential to improving property tax administration is an upgrading of the quality of the people who perform the assessment function by professionalizing assessment personnel.

A first major step in this direction is to require demonstrated competence of all assessors, whether elected or appointed, before they are entrusted with assessing responsibilities. Some progress along these lines has already been made. New Jersey, for example, has just adopted a law providing for the qualification, certification, and examination of tax assessors. This law applies to both elected and appointed assessors and gives assessors the option of either taking an examination or completing state-sponsored assessor in-service training courses to qualify for the tax assessor certificate, which will be required for reappointment or re-election beginning July 1, 1971. Somewhat similar laws have been enacted in a few other states. The New Jersey law also contains provisions whereby tax assessors may gain tenure of office, another essential element in upgrading the professional status of assessing in the United States.

It is equally clear that adequate salaries, career opportunities, and training programs must be provided if the professional standards of assessing personnel are to be raised. One of the prime movers in this field has been the assessors' professional organization, the International Association of Assessing Officers. Accomplishments, while too numerous to detail here, include sponsorship of specific training programs and conferences, publication of practical assessing texts, and a program of professional certification. The association also has set up a special education fund to expand its assessor training programs and develop instructional material which will make it possible for any interested assessor to attain a professional level of assessing skill. Many states offer some in-service training to their local assessors, though not all have been equally useful or productive.

In my opinion, much more would be realized from such in-service training efforts if they were made an integral part of a career development program for assessors. The District of Columbia is now in the process of developing such a program to foster individual growth and develop a high degree of competence and professionalization within its assessing staff. As a first step in developing this program, we defined the total requirements of the assessing staff and established the duties and standards of performance at the various levels of job responsibility. By matching these duties and standards against the background and experience of the individuals in the jobs, we were able to determine our deficiencies and training needs. A program of training and development which involves both formal instruction and on-the-job experience is now being prepared to meet these needs.

Such a career development program provides several major organizational benefits. It enhances the ability of the assessing office to attract able people to its staff and provides the members of the assessing staff a valuable incentive for self-development. Such a program provides the administrator an accurate analysis of development needs with which to plan his training efforts and puts him in a much better position to evaluate his present organization and make needed changes in job positions and staffing.

Substantial improvement in property tax administration is not likely to be made without recognition of the problem of organization and management. The external and internal organizational problems, which are hampering the proper functioning of this important source of local tax revenue, cannot be ignored nor can remedial action be delayed. It is hoped that the states will realize the importance of this and act without further undue delay to remove the legislative and geographic impediments to effective property tax administration. In this regard, the Advisory Commission on Intergovernmental Relations strongly urged in its report:

> No assessment district should be less than countywide and when, as in very many instances, counties are too small to comprise efficient districts, multicounty districts should be created.
> All overlapping assessment districts should be abolished to eliminate wasteful duplication of work.[3]

Local assessment officials have an equally vital role to perform in improving their internal organizational structure and operations. Any assessing office can improve its management by constant and vigorous attention to such matters as setting meaningful goals and objectives, measuring the degree to which these are accomplished, keeping its organization sufficiently vital to meet the objectives, making analyses of organizational strength, creating a climate that rewards constructive effort, offering opportunities for professional development, motivating people, and appraising the value of the service it provides. This is a big order but not outside the realm of possibility.

Although major improvements take time, much can be done within the present limitations of most existing laws and budgets. A more effective job can be performed by further refining mass appraisal techniques and utilizing automatic data processing more fully. Practically all assessing offices could achieve better overall assessment equality by streamlining their present procedures to reduce the appalling waste of their limited supply of valuable appraisal skills. More time and effort of experienced assessors should be devoted to analysis of land values, appraisal of large and complex properties, and study of the real estate market as a whole rather than to the making of many minor adjustments in the assessment of residential and farm buildings.

There is no single or simple solution to improving property tax administration. Our challenge is to make the property tax a workable and reliable source of revenue for local government. Organizational improvement is one of the key factors for accomplishing this objective.

Notes

1 A. M. Woodruff and L. L. Ecker-Racz, "Property Taxes and Land Use Patterns in Australia and New Zealand," *The Tax Executive,* XVIII, No. 1 (October, 1965), 16–63.

2 James R. Vine, "The Role and Responsibility of the Assessor," *Tax Policy,* XXXIII, No. 12 (December, 1966), 5–6.

3 Advisory Commission on Intergovernmental Relations, *The Role of the States in Strengthening the Property Tax* (Washington, D.C., 1963), p. 15.

John D. Cole II

The Effect of Electronic Data Processing upon Property Tax Administration

Few inventions of mankind are more brilliant in concept than the electronic computer. The speed at which these machines handle complex mathematical equations or millions of pieces of information is staggering. Thousands of computers and data handling devices are in daily use in industry and government, presumably saving someone great chunks of time, human effort, and money.

Local property tax administrators view this activity and undoubtedly wonder about utilizing computers to aid in the solution of their problems. Obviously, there are benefits tax administrators can draw from electronic data processing, but we urge these officials to proceed with caution lest they fall into the same pitfalls that have caught other data processing users. By no means are all computer systems successful. Failures are difficult to document because lack of success with a computer is rarely revealed to the outside world, but they are there nonetheless.

Computers are not a panacea for all of man's problems any more than other devices are. Most unsuccessful computer installations fail to live up to expectations because the decisions leading to their acquisition were not soberly and carefully thought out. These decisions are sometimes made in haste, overly influenced by the tug of emotions and not enough by a cool reasoning process. Computers, aside from being fantastic machines, have also become status symbols greatly sought after to feed the human ego.

If the decision on when and how to computerize would be based on the same factors used in acquiring other expensive business machines, supported by a detailed feasibility study and not shrouded in an aura of glamour, the chances for an efficient installation would be greatly enhanced. The commitment for a computer should be only part of a larger commitment for a full data processing system, that is, not just a machine but a total system integrating the problem to be solved, the appropriate machine, and the program to solve the problem.

What steps can local government officials take to reduce the likelihood of major error in choosing a data processing system? The first and most important step is to obtain the best available professional advice. The government of a large community should employ a qualified data processing specialist on its staff to spearhead the entire planning process and not wait until the equipment is ready for delivery. Small communities would probably be better advised to retain a professional data processing consultant to aid in the planning phase and hire a technician later to run the system. Either course has its risks, but both are superior to a community's proceeding on its own by trying to decide on the basis of "common sense" or acting on the advice of a computer salesman.

Few single governmental departments in any community have enough volume of work to justify a computer. The usual practice is for the departments to band together, combine all their present and anticipated needs into one plan, and establish a computer center that will serve all of them. Coordination of this plan—studying all the operations various departments want computerized, shunting aside those of an impractical nature, programming, and establishing the priority for each operation—demands an exceptional man in charge.

There is always a strong tendency to computerize every

operation in every department. From our own data processing experience we can relate that many operations can be performed more efficiently by less glamorous means, such as pencil and paper or desk calculator. This is most often true of low-volume items where special computer programming or machine time involved in compiling and testing the program consumes any savings resulting from computer speed.

Shifting to a more positive note, for there are undeniable advantages to a properly conceived program, let us explore how the computer can benefit local property tax administration. The careful definition of any problem undoubtedly helps in its solution, and the assessor and tax collector do have their problems. The problems are in two areas: those related to applying the present assessments to the task of levying, billing, collecting, and accounting for money needed to run the local government; and those related to improving the basic fairness of the assessments to the taxpayers of the community. These problem areas are tied most closely to the ability of the computer to process vast quantities of data, with somewhat less emphasis on answering complex mathematical questions. Data handling and storage are at the root of the problems; computing is of secondary importance because the mathematics of a sound equalization and tax administration program are not extremely complex, but there is a tremendous number of repetitions of a few relatively simple equations.

Any assessment administrator can now automate the full range of his basic accounting duties: the preparation of the community's official annual tax roll showing ownership, property description, and the assessed values for each individual property; the preparation of forms for tax billing by applying the appropriate tax rate to each property on the tax roll; and the reconciliation of tax payments against the billing, making quickly available the totals of money collected and tax delinquency lists. These steps merely automate the routine clerical paperwork, definitely speeding up the process and possibly saving some money. This procedure is no longer revolutionary, as it is actually being done in many communities.

Going beyond the accounting function of property tax administration and into the valuation area opens the door to a number of electronic data processing applications. My remarks will be confined to four areas: the mass computation of individual appraisals; a continuing statistical study to test the quality of assessments; the annual reappraisal concept; and the data bank concept.

In the computation of appraisals, our firm has led the way, having used computers for almost ten years to compute well over two million individual real estate appraisals for local tax purposes. During this period several competitors have come into the data processing arena to do battle with us. Their basic premise has been that the more complex the system, the better the results. Their lack of success comes very close to proving this premise wrong.

It appears that some major communities doing their own valuation work are now making the same erroneous assumption. A reasonable level of sophistication in an appraisal system is desirable. Up to a point, more complexity does fine-tune an appraisal, but then the law of diminishing returns sets in with a vengeance. Those who forget that appraisals are now and always will be the opinions of men, and perhaps never will be truly scientific, quickly add so much complexity to their system that the appraiser's attention is diverted from the essential elements of valuation to focus on trivial details. This diversion leads inevitably to poor and inconsistent results.

Equity for all taxpayers is extremely important, and, as the local property tax burden increases, equitable treatment becomes increasingly important. Without the existence of basic equity in the tax system, the voters of many communities have stopped passing tax increases for school needs or upgraded services. If provoked further, the voters may, by group action, quit paying their property taxes to force reform.

No matter how impressive a data processing system for tax valuation looks on paper, if it does not yield fair and equitable values based on the prices paid in the market place, it is a failure. Only good appraisers, properly supervised and working with a standardized but flexible appraisal system, can give equitable results.

How can the equity of results be judged? A statistical survey can sample assessments to check the quality and level of a new appraisal program, and also can continue to monitor the trends in each following year. This system can signal when inequities again make a complete reappraisal necessary. Data processing can be a definite aid in this statistical analysis.

Any statistical study of assessment quality must be based on a comparison of market values and assessed values. This process is widely referred to as a sales ratio study. The market value data for a sales ratio study comes from actual sales in the market, screened in the field for accuracy. Sales that are not "arms-length" transactions or that are forced in any way do not represent market value and must be discarded.

The simplest and most often used statistical assessment test is to compare the grand total of prices paid for all the selected sales to the grand total of the assessed values on the same properties. Unfortunately this test proves very little. The flaw is that half the properties sampled might be badly overassessed and the other half badly underassessed, but the overall average could still show the exact prescribed percentage of assessment. This would indicate equalization perfection when obviously that is not the case. More sophisticated statistical measurements can be used to avoid this deception.

The important things to find are how well the properties are equalized and what is the common level of assessment expressed in terms of percentage of market value. Statistical measurements such as the median assessment percentage, the average deviation from the median assessment percentage, and the coefficient of dispersion are very valuable in testing the quality of equalization. These tests require extensive data, particularly if the community is sizable. Computerization of these tests is the obvious solution. Not only can a computer handle a study of the total community's assessments, but it can also analyze neighborhoods to identify areas of inequality that might be corrected on a spot basis.

Once reasonable equity is achieved, there is still a constant battle to maintain fair treatment for even a few years, because market values are constantly in flux. No assessor can maintain reasonable equity for even most taxpayers beyond a few years, perhaps not more than five or six, without a complete revaluation of all properties. This is so because values even for neighboring properties do not generally move as a group but ebb and flow on an individual basis governed, in the case of residential properties, largely by the ever-changing likes and dislikes of the buying public.

Another factor with great impact on value is individual maintenance. The passage of a few years can bring out major differences in value in a neighborhood of basically identical homes. This results from the individual owners' varying policies in caring for their properties. The only solution to the inevitable changes in value is periodic complete revaluation, with every property being viewed by a competent appraiser. Yet many communities, contemplating data processing systems for assessment work, are naive enough to claim their system so modern and up-to-date that it will, by some magic formula, pull out and update properties needing adjustment without their being viewed in the field. These communities seek to eliminate the expense of a personal inspection and appraisal merely by plugging into the computer certain cost factors or market trends.

There is now frequent talk of continuous revaluation programs either by the so-called annual reappraisal method or by dividing the community into several sections, reappraising one section each year, and updating the assessments of each section as reappraisal is completed. The annual reappraisal is now technically feasible through the computer, but it is not economically feasible because of the cost of actually viewing and appraising each property every year. The concept of appraising a different section of the community each year on a relatively short cycle will work, but officials must recognize that this system almost always penalizes those properties last adjusted because the trend of inflation in our economy puts them on a continually higher dollar basis than those appraised in prior years.

Another relatively new concept of possible interest to tax administrators is the community data bank. This is a coordinated effort by all local government agencies to establish and maintain a huge computerized file of data showing the continuing economic, legal, and social history of a community and the individuals living there. Community planners and administrators would be able to call on this file for quick access to data regarding specific problems. For example, statistics on the frequency and location of crimes, accidents, or fires would be very useful in planning for public safety. The age and number of children in each household would help school boards anticipate future needs. Real property data would be helpful in many phases of community planning—zoning, transportation, sanitation, and urban renewal, to name but a few—and conceivably the assessor's basic property record file could be integrated into the data bank for the benefit of other agencies. The potential benefits from an application of this system to local tax administration, however, are unclear at this time.

In summary, the effect of data processing on local tax administration is potentially beneficial if the system is intelligently conceived and carefully developed. The present accounting function of tax administration can be completely automated. Mass appraising can be successfully computerized if the system is specifically designed to retain the element of human opinion and not set to grind out arbitrary answers based on a multitude of theoretical input factors. A thorough annual check on the quality of assessments can be achieved by an automated statistical analysis of sales and assessments. The concepts of annual reappraisals and the data bank are, at the present stage of development, of questionable benefit to local tax administration. On balance, however, the outlook is bright for data processing to help improve the quality of our administration of the local property tax.

5 *Paul V. Corusy*

Improved Property Tax Administration:
Legislative Opportunities and Probabilities

Nearly everyone professes to be an expert on property taxation, and a number of these experts have written books and articles suggesting how it can be reformed. It is significant to note that most of these books and articles use the word "reform" and not the word "abolish." Twenty years ago other experts were advocating abolition of the property tax and replacement of the lost revenue from other sources. To support abolition of the tax, this movement reasoned, first, that revenue from property taxes could be replaced from other sources without major disruption to the economy, and, second, that the property tax was almost impossible to administer and, therefore, should be abolished.

Conditions have changed. Today, revenue from property taxes is over $25,000,000,000 annually, and is exceeded only by the federal income tax on corporate and individual income. Replacing property tax revenue with moneys from other sources would indeed present many complex problems today, and it is doubtful that such could be accomplished without disrupting the economy of most local governments. In fact, no reasonable or palatable substitute tax has been advocated that would raise the current return of $25,000,000,000.

TABLE 5.1

ANNUAL SALARIES OF ASSESSING OFFICERS BY STATES AND PROVINCES, 1966

State	No. of assessing officers*	Average salary Rank	Average salary Amount ($)	Lowest salary ($)	Highest salary ($)
Alabama	21	16	$ 8,143	$ 3,600	$17,000
Alaska	7	1	13,227	11,000	15,000
Arizona	14	15	8,429	7,200	10,400
Arkansas	75	49	4,547	2,700	5,000
California	62	3	12,192	4,800	35,000
Colorado	63	41	5,203	2,760	11,772
Connecticut	70	19	8,013	3,000	14,534
Delaware	2	17	8,122	7,245	9,000
Florida	76	9	9,758	4,800	14,839
Georgia	6	11	9,418	6,300	14,924
Hawaii	5	6	10,382	9,096	11,616
Idaho	44	42	5,198	3,036	8,000
Illinois	53	28	6,887	3,600	9,900
Indiana	2	20	8,000	6,000	10,000
Iowa	117	31	6,555	4,400	14,200
Kansas	5	34	6,199	5,200	7,350
Kentucky	122	39	5,799	3,000	7,200
Louisiana	70	8	10,119	5,400	15,000
Maine	21	30	6,571	3,000	10,500
Maryland	24	7	10,249	6,200	18,445
Massachusetts	17	12	9,091	6,600	15,000
Michigan	57	13	8,842	5,200	17,894
Minnesota	92	29	6,708	3,000	15,300
Mississippi	82	45	4,843	4,200	5,500
Missouri	2	2	12,564	9,900	15,228
Montana	56	50	4,434	3,650	6,300
Nebraska	80	48	4,634	3,600	10,000
Nevada	16	22	7,775	5,900	12,000
New Hampshire	3	18	8,100	5,800	9,500
New Jersey	91	24	7,548	3,400	16,064
New Mexico	31	40	5,783	2,750	7,920
New York	20	4	11,370	3,400	25,000
North Carolina	36	35	6,087	3,000	11,000
North Dakota	7	21	7,944	4,500	11,304
Ohio	86	26	7,352	4,500	16,000
Oklahoma	77	47	4,640	3,270	10,915
Oregon	36	25	7,393	4,200	14,500
Pennsylvania	4	33	6,405	4,200	8,700
Rhode Island	4	27	7,005	5,500	8,000

TABLE 5.1 (cont.)

State	No. of assessing officers*	Average salary Rank	Average salary Amount ($)	Lowest salary ($)	Highest salary ($)
South Carolina	2	10	9,600	9,600	9,600
South Dakota	70	43	5,140	3,300	8,976
Tennessee	89	44	4,865	3,200	15,000
Texas	67	14	8,448	3,840	20,000
Utah	21	36	6,014	4,800	10,000
Vermont	7	32	6,500	5,000	8,800
Virginia	20	5	11,102	6,000	17,700
Washington	39	37	5,951	3,700	12,000
West Virginia	55	46	4,792	2,800	8,100
Wisconsin	65	23	7,631	2,700	21,006
Wyoming	23	38	5,843	4,800	6,600
OVERALL, United States	2,114		6,848	2,700	35,000
Alberta	2	4	7,900	7,200	8,600
British Columbia	49	5	7,357	4,200	12,756
Manitoba	1	1	16,800	16,800	16,800
New Brunswick	5	6	7,260	6,200	9,000
Ontario	10	2	11,580	7,100	24,000
Quebec	6	3	9,211	8,500	10,000
OVERALL, Canada	73		8,225	4,200	24,000
OVERALL, United States and Canada	2,187		6,894	2,700	35,000

* Based on International Association of Assessing Officers survey.

From the large amount of revenue obtained, it must be assumed that the property tax *is* possible to administer; in the words of A. M. Woodruff, Chancellor of the University of Hartford, a recognized expert in property taxation, "Despite the double-barrelled handicap of geographic dispersion and relatively untrained personnel, the property tax has worked, not as well as it could and far less well than it should, but nevertheless it has worked. The fact that it works at all under these handicaps is strong testimony that it is essentially a very simple tax to administer."[1]

In forty-nine of our fifty states, the overall assessing function is vested in local assessing agencies. Yet from one state to another, the property tax may differ, both in what the laws specify and in what assessment administrators actually do. Regardless of these differences, the primary purpose of property tax administration in all areas is the determination of the value of the taxable property of each taxpayer, so that each taxpayer will bear fairly his proportion of the overall levy.

The proper administration of these functions, however, has been limited in varying degrees by poor property tax laws, of which three problem areas are most noticeable.

1. Too often the position of the assessor, along with the operation of his office, has been relegated to one of minor importance. Thus, in far too many instances, competent administration is being limited through inadequate office budgets, lack of tenure, and low salary levels. A state or local jurisdiction will pay thousands of dollars to a fee appraiser for condemnation appraisal purposes, yet will pay only a fraction of that amount to maintain, supposedly, the entire office of the assessor (see Table 5.1). However, the American taxpayer has been fortunate that, even with these limitations, a growing number of professionally competent personnel are administering this important function.

2. Outmoded and sometimes unworkable property tax laws are found in most states, and, even though such laws may not be enforced or administered, they nevertheless remain law. To add to the confusion of administration, the laws may be written whereby either they contain great detail as to their administration, or they are broad in scope, creating difficulties as to what is or is not applicable under the law. In either instance, certain problems or difficulties complicate the achievement of competent administration.

3. Minimum qualifications for the position of assessor are nonexistent in most of the states. This does not imply that many elected or appointed assessors are not qualified for their position. Indeed, a significant number of assessors have earned professional designations such as CAE, MAI, and SREA, which indicate to some degree their professional competence.

Nonetheless, the group of professional assessors constitutes a small percentage of the total, and the problem thus remains to adopt or, in some instances, to upgrade the qualifications for the position of assessor.

These are only three of the major areas of concern associated with effective property tax administration. The time has long passed for those concerned with assessment administration to remain in a state of complacency. Within the past five years there have been significant measures enacted by legislators toward improving property tax administration which are worthy of consideration and possible adoption by other states.

Measures to Improve Property Tax Administration

There has been considerable activity by the state legislatures in the property tax area since 1966. States such as Georgia, Maryland, Missouri, Tennessee, Alabama, and Arkansas have established special legislative study commissions within the last three years to review the total property tax structure and develop recommendations for its improvement. Other states such as Colorado, Indiana, Oklahoma, Oregon, New Hampshire, South Carolina, and South Dakota have permanent legislative tax study committees which include among their functions the continual study of the property tax system.

The recommended improvements in property taxation from these committees have not always resulted in far-reaching changes; nevertheless, the changes which have been adopted have resulted in improved property tax administration. Most noticeable of the advances being made today are in the areas of the qualification of the assessor and size of his jurisdiction, and the revision of outmoded and sometimes unworkable property tax laws.

Assessor Qualifications

According to a report issued by the U.S. Bureau of the Census in 1966, there are more than 14,000 primary assessing areas in the United States. But this figure would double in size if all assessing jurisdictions were included. An analysis of the census report shows that slightly more than 50 percent of the assessors in these primary areas are elected as compared to 25 percent who are appointed. The remaining 24 percent are from jurisdictions which allow the assessor to be either elected or appointed (see Table 5.2) .

Regardless of whether the assessor is elected or appointed, most states have not established minimal requirements for this position. Thus, in many jurisdictions, especially the smaller ones from the standpoint of property values, it is possible for a person to hold this position even though his knowledge of appraising property may be extremely limited. Nevertheless, as noted before, there are a number of highly qualified assessors, as witnessed by the many who have obtained national and state professional designations. This nucleus of professional assessors, whose numbers are ever increasing, has been a forceful voice in advocating minimum qualifications for all assessors (see Table 5.3) .

The movement toward increasing the professional qualifications of assessors has been initiated mainly through the efforts of various state and national assessor organizations, and not through state legislation. Several states, including New York and Nebraska, have considered the desirability of establishing minimum qualifications but have been unable to pass appropriate legislation. Five states—Oregon, California, New Jersey, Tennessee, and Kansas—have been successful in establishing certain statewide qualifications for assessors.

Oregon was the first state with such legislation in 1955. That law states, "Appraisals of real property made after January 1, 1957, shall be performed by a certified appraiser." The State Tax Commission was empowered to determine the necessary qualifications for a certified appraiser.

During 1966–67 California, New Jersey, and Tennessee passed statewide certification legislation, and Kansas passed such legislation in 1968. In 1966, California enacted bill AB80, which included many sections toward improving the property tax system in the state. One section of the act pertains to appraiser qualifications and states, "Every state and county prop-

TABLE 5.2

PRIMARY ASSESSING AREAS ACCORDING TO METHOD USED FOR SELECTING ASSES-
SORS, BY STATE

State and type of government	Number of primary assessing areas*	Method for selecting assessors		
		Appointed	Appointed and elected	Elected
Alabama, Total	67			
Counties		—	—	67
Alaska, Total	29			
Boroughs		9	—	—
Municipalities		19	—	—
School Districts		1	—	—
Arizona, Total	14			
Counties		—	—	14
Arkansas, Total	75			
Counties		—	—	75
California, Total	58			
Counties		—	—	58
Colorado, Total	63			
Counties		—	—	63
Connecticut, Total	169			
Municipalities		—	19	—
Towns		—	150	—
Delaware, Total	3			
Counties		3	—	—
District of Columbia, Total	1			
Municipalities		1	—	—
Florida, Total	67			
Counties		—	—	67
Georgia, Total	159			
Counties		159	—	—
Hawaii, Total	1			
State		1	—	—
Idaho, Total	44			
Counties		—	—	44
Illinois, Total	1,424			
Counties		—	—	20
Municipalities		—	—	4
Townships		—	—	1,400
Indiana, Total	1,009			
Townships		—	—	1,009
Iowa, Total	120			
Counties		99	—	—
Municipalities		21	—	—

TABLE 5.2 (cont.)

State and type of government	Number of primary assessing areas*	Method for selecting assessors		
		Appointed	Appointed and elected	Elected
Kansas, Total	105			
Counties		—	—	105
Kentucky, Total	120			
Counties		—	—	120
Louisiana, Total	64			
Parishes		—	—	64
Maine, Total	492			
State		1	—	—
Municipalities		21	—	—
Towns		470	—	—
Maryland, Total	24			
Counties		—	24	—
Massachusetts, Total	351			
Municipalities		—	39	—
Towns		—	312	—
Michigan, Total	1,475			
Municipalities		—	216	—
Townships		—	—	1,259
Minnesota, Total	721			
Counties		70	—	—
Municipalities		218	—	—
Townships		433	—	—
Mississippi, Total	82			
Counties		—	—	82
Missouri, Total	435			
Counties		—	90	—
Municipalities		1	—	—
Townships		—	—	344
Montana, Total	56			
Counties		—	—	56
Nebraska, Total	93			
Counties		—	—	93
Nevada, Total	17			
Counties		—	—	17
New Hampshire, Total	234			
Municipalities		—	13	—
Townships		—	—	221
New Jersey, Total	567			
Municipalities		—	334	—

TABLE 5.2 (cont.)

| State and type of government | Number of primary assessing areas* | Method for selecting assessors | | |
		Appointed	Appointed and elected	Elected
Townships		—	233	—
New Mexico, Total	32			
Counties		—	—	32
New York, Total	990			
Counties		1	—	—
Municipalities		60	—	—
Towns		929	—	—
North Carolina, Total	100			
Counties		100	—	—
North Dakota, Total	1,772			
Counties		—	—	29
Municipalities		356	—	—
Townships		—	—	1,387
Ohio, Total	88			
Counties		—	—	88
Oklahoma, Total	77			
Counties		—	—	77
Oregon, Total	36			
Counties		—	—	36
Pennsylvania, Total	67			
Counties		67	—	—
Rhode Island, Total	39			
Municipalities		—	8	—
Towns		—	31	—
South Carolina, Total	46			
Counties		46	—	—
South Dakota, Total	404			
Counties		51	—	—
Municipalities		87	—	—
Townships		266	—	—
Tennessee, Total	95			
Counties		—	—	95
Texas, Total	254			
Counties		—	—	254
Utah, Total	29			
Counties		—	—	29
Vermont, Total	246			
Municipalities		—	8	—
Towns		—	238	—

TABLE 5.2 (cont.)

State and type of government	Number of primary assessing areas*	Method for selecting assessors		
		Appointed	Appointed and elected	Elected
Virginia, Total	131			
Counties		98	—	—
Municipalities		33	—	—
Washington, Total	39			
Counties		—	—	39
West Virginia, Total	55			
Counties		—	—	55
Wisconsin, Total	1,834			
Municipalities		—	563	—
Towns		—	1,271	—
Wyoming, Total	23			
Counties		—	—	23
TOTAL	14,496	3,621	3,549	7,326
PERCENTAGE	100%	25%	24%	51%

* Based on U.S. Bureau of the Census, *Primary Assessing Areas for Local Property Taxation*, April, 1966.

erty tax appraiser will be required to have a valid appraiser's certificate issued by the State Board of Equalization demonstrating a competence to perform his duties. Applicants must pass an examination administered or approved by the Board. Those performing audit functions for property tax purposes must hold degrees in accounting from recognized institutions of higher education, or be licensed to practice accounting in California, or have passed a state or county civil service examination for accountant or auditor. Elected assessors are exempt from these requirements."

Although California has exempted elected assessors from these requirements, New Jersey has included them in its certification bill and requires that no assessor, after July 1, 1971, may be appointed or elected unless he holds a tax assessor certificate. The only exception to this certification is any assessor who will have served continuously in office from July 1, 1967, and is reappointed or re-elected to the position. Another sec-

TABLE 5.3

STATE AND NATIONAL PROFESSIONAL DESIGNATIONS AVAILABLE TO ASSESSORS AND
APPRAISERS

ASA	American Society of Appraisers
SIR	Society of Industrial Realtors
CRE	Council of Real Estate
AACI	Accredited Appraisers–Canadian Institute
CAE	IAAO Certified Assessment Evaluator
CCA	Certified Connecticut Assessor
SMA	Society of Municipal Assessors (New Jersey)
IAO	Institute of Assessing Officers (New York)
CSDA	Certified South Dakota Assessor
CTA	Certified Texas Assessor
CTA	Certified Tax Appraiser (Colorado)
CIAO	Certified Illinois Assessing Officer
CIA	Certified Iowa Assessor
CMA	Certified Minnesota Assessor
NSIA	Nova Scotia Institute of Assessors
AIMA	Associate of the Institute of Municipal Assessors (Ontario)
MIMA	Member of the Institute of Municipal Assessors (Ontario)
FIMA	Fellowship of the Institute of Municipal Assessors (Ontario)
CMA	Certified Massachusetts Assessor
MIE	Member Institute des Estimateurs (Quebec)
AIE	Aspirant Institute des Estimateurs (Quebec)
MAI	Member of American Institute
SRA	Senior Residential Appraiser
SREA	Senior Real Estate Appraiser

tion contained in the New Jersey law but not found in the California law is that the applicant shall provide satisfactory proof that he ". . . has obtained a certificate or diploma issued after at least 4 years of study in an approved secondary school or has received an academic education considered and accepted by the Commissioner of Education as fully equivalent, and has graduated from a 4-year course at a college of recognized standing. An applicant who does not meet the college education requirement may substitute full-time experience in real estate appraisal work or experience in property tax assessment work on a year-for-year basis."

Tennessee law does not include minimum education requirements, but like New Jersey it does require certification of elected assessors: "To assure that the assessment functions will be performed in a professional manner by competent assessors, meeting clearly specified professional qualifications, the State Board of Equalization is authorized and directed to prescribe educational and training courses to be taken by assessors and their deputies, and to specify qualification requirements for certification of anyone who is to be engaged to appraise and assess property for the purpose of taxation." The legislation further provides that after 1972 all municipal and other assessment offices will be consolidated into the office of a county assessor. The county assessors shall be elected every four years, except in counties where, by a vote of the people, it has been determined to have an appointed assessor; and any county containing less than the minimum number of parcels (to be determined by the State Tax Commission) for efficient and appropriate administration may contract with an adjoining county to create a jurisdiction large enough to justify the employment of a competent professional appraiser and staff.

Although varying in their approaches, California, New Jersey, Tennessee, Oregon, and Kansas are the leaders in providing for certification at the state level. Another factor common to all is the reference to training programs.

Training Programs

All states have some type of training program. These programs may be held for one day or they may extend to two weeks. The material may be presented in a formal classroom atmosphere or it may consist of discussion sessions on specific topics. Whether or not many of these programs can be substantiated as training programs sometimes remains a debatable question. What is not disputed is the fact that specifically designed courses for assessor training have been developed and are made available to assessors throughout the country.

The International Association of Assessing Officers has been actively engaged in conducting training programs since 1965. Courses of instruction for differing levels of achievement have been established, supplemental material to the text has been prepared, and an examination is given at the completion of each course. Qualified professional assessors, who have proved their ability to teach others, are used as instructors for the courses.

Legislative provisions have been made to establish schools for assessors in Tennessee, Florida, Illinois, and Kansas, and similar programs are being considered in Alabama.

Certification and training programs are extremely important in the improvement of property tax administration. However, if the assessor is compelled to administer outmoded or unworkable laws, then only partial success can be expected.

Property Tax Laws

Changes in property tax laws are continually being made during the various state legislative sessions. The majority of these laws are concerned primarily with clarifying existing laws and providing various types of property tax relief.

Within the general area of clarifying existing laws, equalization has received much attention. Georgia, Arizona, and Nebraska are striving for uniformity through statewide reassessment programs which are near completion; New Mexico is in the initial stage of its program.

The courts also have been active in the area of equalization, regarding primarily the use of fractional valuations among various classes of property within a state and those valuations in use which differ from what is specified in state statutes. Statutes in twenty-three states require assessment of property generally at full value. In seventeen states the statutes specify a flat percentage of full value, and Hawaii has done so by administrative policy. In Minnesota, Montana, and Arizona, property is classified by statute, with various percentages applying to different classes of property. In six states—Connecticut, New Jersey, North Carolina, Louisiana, Rhode Island, and Vermont—the percentage at which property is assessed varies among jurisdictions and is determined locally. Maine requires that property be assessed at "just value" and Wyoming at "a fair value."

Although the statutes in twenty-three states require assessment at full value, only three states are presently at that level.

Florida and Kentucky made the change as a result of court decisions. In May, 1967, the Governor of Oregon signed into law Senate Bill 9 which requires that all property in the state be assessed at 100 percent of "true cash value" instead of the current 25 percent. Oregon thus became the first state to effect such a change through legislation (see Table 5.4).

TABLE 5.4

STATUTORY ASSESSMENT RATIOS FOR TANGIBLE PROPERTY, BY STATE, JUNE, 1968

Alabama	30	Montana	‡
Alaska	100	Nebraska	35
Arizona	‡	Nevada	35
Arkansas	20	New Hampshire	100
California	25	New Jersey	20–100 *
Colorado	30	New Mexico	100
Connecticut	up to 100 *	New York	100
Delaware	100	North Carolina	*
Florida	100	North Dakota	50
Georgia	100	Ohio	50
Hawaii	70 †	Oklahoma	35
Idaho	20	Oregon	100
Illinois	100	Pennsylvania	100
Indiana	33⅓	Rhode Island	not to exceed 100 *
Iowa	27	South Carolina	100
Kansas	30	South Dakota	60
Kentucky	100	Tennessee	50
Louisiana	not below 25 *	Texas	100
Maine	just value	Utah	30
Maryland	100	Vermont	*
Massachusetts	100	Virginia	100
Michigan	50	Washington	50
Minnesota	‡	West Virginia	100
Mississippi	100	Wisconsin	100
Missouri	100	Wyoming	a fair value

* Uniform percentage determined locally.
† By administrative policy.
‡ Various classifications.

Idaho's classification of property with its various percentages was declared unconstitutional, and a uniform ratio of 20 percent has now been established. In California the voters approved a uniform ratio of 25 percent in 1966. A Georgia court recently held that no longer could public utility property be classified and assessed at a higher ratio than other property within the state.

It is evident from these few examples that the *status quo* no longer will be accepted, at least from the court's viewpoint, where equalization is concerned. If the states, through the various means at their disposal, are unwilling to achieve equalization, the courts have not been reluctant to assume the responsibility.

The second area receiving much attention is exempt property. In the United States the power to exempt property rests with the state, and it is this area of exemptions where the greatest number of variations exist. One of the major premises for providing exemptions is that certain institutions and organizations exert positive influences in the community whereby the benefits received by the community far outweigh the revenue which may be obtained. This premise, as practiced, receives various treatments among the states, and it is not unusual to examine comparable properties and find that in one state the property is taxed under a strict interpretation of the law while in another state the same type of property may receive liberal benefits. For example, Maryland exempts all religious property, but in Texas only that portion used for conducting religious services and one residence for the minister is exempt. To compound the confusion, the law exempting certain property may be so broad in scope that it creates difficulties as to what is or is not applicable under the law.

Within the last two decades, and more especially in the last six years, the amount of property removed from the tax rolls has been increasing at a rapid pace. More than one-third of the states in 1967 considered various broad proposals for property tax relief for certain classes of property or taxpayers (see Table 5.5).

Various private and governmental organizations have estimated the value of exempt property in the United States, but, at best, the valuations remain only estimates because most states do not attempt to place a value on exempt property. Even for the few states that do make an attempt, the data are usually confined to only certain types of exemptions. Although the data are incomplete, they are useful in that they give some

TABLE 5.5

PROPERTY TAX RELIEF PROPOSALS IN GOVERNORS' MESSAGES IN 1967 *

| State | General | | | | Personal property | | | |
	Credits	State aid	Rate limit	Other	Inventories	Other	Aged persons	State rate
California	x	x	—	—	—	—	—	—
Colorado	—	x	—	—	—	—	—	—
Connecticut	—	—	—	—	—	—	x	—
Idaho	—	—	—	—	x	—	—	—
Indiana	—	—	—	x	—	—	—	—
Iowa	—	—	—	—	—	x	x	—
Kansas	—	—	—	—	—	—	x	—
Maryland	—	x	—	—	x	—	x	x
Michigan	x	—	—	—	—	—	—	—
Minnesota	—	x	—	x	x	—	x	x
Montana	—	—	—	x	—	—	—	—
Nebraska	—	—	—	—	—	x	—	—
North Dakota	—	—	—	—	—	x	—	—
Ohio	—	—	—	—	—	—	x	—
Oregon	—	x	x	—	—	—	—	—
Utah	—	—	—	x	x	—	—	—
Washington	—	—	x	—	—	—	—	—
Wisconsin	—	—	—	x	—	—	—	—
Wyoming	—	—	—	—	x	—	—	—

* Federation of Tax Administrators, "Property Tax Relief Proposals Figure Prominently in Legislative Considerations," *Tax Administrators News*, April, 1967, p. 1.

indication of the minimum value of the properties that are exempt. In Louisiana, for example, the value of industrial and homestead exemptions is equivalent to more than 79 percent of the assessed value of all taxable property. All exempt property, including federal, in the District of Columbia is equivalent to more than 40 percent of all taxable property; in Hawaii it is more than 18 percent; and in Ohio it is more than 10 percent. For New Jersey and South Dakota the value of all exempt property, except federal, is equivalent to more than 15 percent of all taxable property in each state.

These few statistics are enlightening and somewhat startling, yet the continual erosion of the tax base through exemptions continues. The exempt process is still used in an effort to cure or solve social and economic problems, and it is being increasingly applied as a convenient method for dealing with some of the administrative problems in property taxation. Unfortunately, the attempts in many instances have been stopgap measures, have achieved only partial success, and have created far more problems in administration than they were supposed to cure.

Measures requiring certification and training of assessors, the enactment of new laws, and the clarification of existing laws have decidedly improved property tax administration. The property tax system will continue to need improvement, but its advancement will depend largely upon the leadership of state governments.

Probabilities of Property Tax Administration

The progress being made to improve property tax administration is not readily discernible to all. It is understandable that certain individuals or organizations clamor for more rapid advancement, but it is a peculiarity of our political system that change generally takes place at a snail's pace. Despite this, various trends are emerging which will result in dramatic improvement of property tax administration.

Since the early 1950's heavy demands have been placed on state and local governments to provide additional services and expand existing ones. For the local governments, at least, a major portion of the revenue is obtained from local property taxes, and other revenue sources are oftentimes limited. The local governments have been compelled to seek reforms or more equitable allocation of tax revenue, but taxpayers in many communities continue to experience rapid increases in their property tax rates. The combination of these elements form the catalyst for change.

Full Disclosure

The core of property tax administration is the valuation of each taxpayer's taxable property, so that each taxpayer will bear fairly his proportionate part of the overall tax levy. But because of a general lack of interest on the part of the taxpayer and the reluctance of some assessment jurisdictions to disclose information, property tax administration is often surrounded in mystery. This coat of mystery is being removed, and, while no state has gone all the way, California's legislation (bill AB80) clearly points the way toward full disclosure. This 1966 legislation directs the local assessor to include the assessment ratio and an estimate of the full cash value of the property on the routine notice of an assessment increase. John Shannon from the Advisory Commission on Intergovernmental Relations has stated,

. . . a full-disclosure policy can be justified on grounds of taxpayer equity and political strategy. If an assessor deviates from the legal valuation standard (full value in a majority of states), property owners have a right to know the approximate fraction of estimated market value that is being used for tax assessment purposes . . . . From the standpoint of political strategy, they [taxpayers] can be expected to be more receptive to a State policy which would enable them to judge the fairness of their own assessment.[2]

Assessors and Assessment Jurisdictions

Within the next decade two important changes will take place. First, we judge that most states by 1980 will require anyone holding the position of assessor to meet certain minimal qualifications and to be certified by some agency. In conjunction with certification will be mandatory training programs established by the state or other organizations approved by the state. Such requirements already exist in legislation passed in California, New Jersey, Kansas, and Tennessee and are being considered in Florida, Alabama, and Illinois.

The second important change will be in the size of assessment jurisdictions. The present multitude of jurisdictions will be significantly reduced, resulting in larger jurisdictions that can be administered by adequately compensated professional assessors and that can provide the necessary office budget and staff for competent administration. Several years ago Iowa reduced the number of jurisdictions within the state from over 1500 to less than 120, and pending legislation in Wisconsin proposes to reduce the number through a county office. The legislation passed in Tennessee is perhaps the best illustration how these changes will be accomplished: all municipal and other assessment jurisdictions are to be combined into one county office; two or more counties may combine to form one assessment jurisdiction under the administration of a professional assessor; and county assessors are elected every four years, except in counties where, by a vote of the people, it has been determined to have an appointed assessor.

Laws

Through the combined efforts of assessor organizations, legislative committees, and taxpayer organizations, property tax laws that are administrable will be passed. "The professional assessor must be provided with a law he can administer, he can live and work with, he can be honest about."[3]

Laws which have not been enforced will be changed or deleted. For example, in nineteen states and the District of Columbia, household personal property is exempt. For the remaining thirty-one states, partial exemptions have been granted, with little revenue collected. Yet forms must be sent and processed by the assessor. A similar situation exists for taxing money and credits. In this particular instance, however, the *ad valorem* tax is being replaced by other forms of taxation. The abolition of taxes on household personal property and on money and credits for *ad valorem* purposes is near.

Tax relief for the elderly, veterans, and other specialized groups is a notable and worthy endeavor. However, this is a social and economic problem and has no relationship to administration of the property tax. If society deems these functions worthwhile, the same objectives can be accomplished through credits on personal income or reimbursements to the local jurisdictions. In Indiana, for example, eight percent of the sales tax revenue is to be returned to the county from which it was collected, and eight percent of individual income tax must be returned to the taxpayer's county of residence.

Exemptions

Although the complete elimination of exempt property is unrealistic, stringent measures are forthcoming as to its use and the amount of property which will be exempt. Many states will join Alabama, Georgia, Missouri, New York, and Tennessee by establishing committees to recommend changes in their tax exempt laws. There will also be an increase in the number of states requiring the assessor to maintain a separate assessment roll for all exempt property, similar to the law passed March, 1967, in South Dakota.

In addition to more stringent controls on exempt property, greater use will be made of in lieu payments. Connecticut and Idaho recently exempted inventories, but the state will reimburse certain portions of the lost revenue to the local jurisdictions. Some states may follow the example of Missouri, which allocates monies to local jurisdictions based on the amount of state land in their area. Or they may follow Wyoming, which allows local governments to finance the construction of industrial development projects and arrange for the payment of rentals and other charges by the lessee. Although the state and federal governments have modest programs providing in lieu payments to local government, these programs will be substantially increased to include many of those agencies which now are exempt. Religious, charitable, and nonprofit organizations will not escape this trend, and they, too, will be required to provide in lieu payments for the services they receive.

State Property Tax

The repeal of the state property tax in Nebraska in November of 1966 foretells the demise of this practice. Currently twenty-three states still levy a state property tax, with fourteen states using the revenue for state purposes. New Mexico and Utah use the revenue for schools, whereas in Ohio it is for soldiers' bonuses. Maryland revenues retire the state's bonded debt, and Minnesota's levy is limited to bond issues of state public building and old constitutional grants. Maine, Utah, and Hawaii redistribute all the revenue to local governments, although Hawaii may be separately classified, as the state is the only agency which administers the property tax. Alabama, Mississippi, Missouri, and Texas return part of the revenue to local governments. Although Colorado, Georgia, Delaware, and South Dakota do not levy a state property tax, each may do so at any time. With the rapid increase of tax bills to the taxpayer and the reliance of local governments on the revenue from property taxes, more and more states are abandoning the state property tax levy and turning to other forms of taxation to raise the necessary revenue (see Table 5.6).

TABLE 5.6

STATES LEVYING A PROPERTY TAX. REVENUE DISTRIBUTION FROM STATE PROPERTY TAX, 1966*

State	State general fund	Distributed to local governments	
		All revenue	Part of revenue
Alabama	—	—	x
Arizona	x	—	—
Hawaii	—	x	—
Idaho	x	—	—
Indiana	no response		
Kansas	x	—	—
Kentucky	x	—	—
Louisiana	x	—	—
Maine	—	x	—
Maryland	x	—	—
Minnesota	x	—	—
Mississippi	—	—	x
Missouri	—	—	x
Montana	x	—	—
Nevada	x	—	—
New Mexico	x	—	—
North Dakota	no response		
Ohio	x	—	—
Texas	—	—	x
Utah	—	x	—
Washington	x	—	—
West Virginia	x	—	—
Wyoming	x	—	—

* International Association of Assessing Officers special survey.

Taxpayers

The role of the taxpayer in good government should not be underestimated. However, before a taxpayer can contribute much toward the betterment of tax administration, he must have a clear concept of the purpose of taxes: he must know and understand that only through taxation can the function of government be accomplished. Too often the taxpayer has been passive in preventing the organized creation of overexaggerated "wants," and one of his almost forgotten roles is the prerogative to ask questions and demand answers about how and for what tax money is being spent. In the future he must make diligent inquiry into the value of many programs and services and determine which should be curtailed or even totally discontinued.

Valuations used in assessing *ad valorem* taxes are primarily factual issues, and facts are infinitely variable. Taxpayers will help eliminate much potential arm's length collision by cooperating with and assisting assessing officials to set up flexible guidelines by the use of rational and acceptable regulations. At times, the modification of certain laws and procedures will be required to maintain local property tax systems that will continue to serve both government and taxpaying community effectively. The average taxpayer cannot be expected to devise laws to improve the assessment of property or the methods of appeal. Nevertheless, he can, with study, knowledge, and advice, assist legislators and administrators in determining what is wrong and how improvements could be made.

The problems of administering tax laws are numerous and sometimes difficult, but not unsolvable. One of the great tasks of the present time is the active participation by all to give new meaning and vitality to the concept of self-government. If we believe the benefits of local government outweigh its burdens, we must protect and sustain it by providing the necessary revenue from local sources for it to operate effectively and efficiently.

The property tax will continue to be of major importance as a source of local revenue. We must be willing to accept changes and to strive diligently for passage of any and all measures which will improve its administration.

Notes

1 "The Perennial Subject of Property Tax Reform," presented at the Annual Conference, International Association of Assessing Officers, September 12, 1966, Toronto, Ontario, Canada.

2 John Shannon, "Full Disclosure Policy—The State's Role in the Assessment Process," presented at Tax Institute of America Symposium, November 2, 1966, Chicago, Illinois.

3 Jacob M. Jaffee, "Property Tax Assessment Reform—A Progress Report," presented at the Annual Meeting, Society of Professional Assessors; printed in the *Maine Townsman*, April, 1967, pp. 7–8.

III. ASSESSMENT
PROCEDURES

Daniel M. Holland and William M. Vaughn

An Evaluation of Self-Assessment under a Property Tax

The tax on real property is one of the oldest and most widely used of government revenue measures. It is reasonable to expect that by now "all the changes" have been rung in administering this type of levy. Understandably, then, self-assessment—the topic of our chapter—is not a revolutionary new idea. Tried in the past and found wanting, it has drifted into the class of administrative devices that are not effective because the sanctions they incorporate are not severe enough to counteract man's deep-set addiction to personal advantage. However, quite recently there has been a lively rebirth of interest in the potential of self-assessment, particularly with reference to a version of the scheme incorporating a new wrinkle that its supporters claim would make it more effective. Under this proposal, they argue, the taxpayer would be faced with a threat that would curb his pursuit of self-interest. In fact, arguing from the results of competitive markets, they assert we would be able to hitch personal material motivation to the common good.

While the proposal relates to a change in how the tax base would be determined, considerably more than some improvement in administration of the property tax has been claimed for it. This new technique has been described by its progenitor as "a simple scheme" which "is self-enforcing, allows no scope for corruption, has negligible costs of administration, and creates incentives, in addition to those already present in the market, for each property to be put to that use in which it has the highest economic productivity."[1] In the muted lexicon of public finance, which usually ranges from "neutral" to "seriously deleterious" in its description of the effects of taxes, these are uncharacteristically laudatory claims. And they contrast strongly too with the typical current characterizations of the property tax even in the best-administered of jurisdictions. Indeed, the potential claimed for this new scheme makes it seem like the fiscal equivalent of the alchemists' "philosopher's stone."

Yet self-assessment, with suitable sanctions, has been put forward as a serious suggestion, not simply as something that someone conjured up. And it is in that spirit that we shall discuss it here. Our chapter, in the main, is a set of speculative reflections on what we see as some of the major problems raised by self-assessment.

The current surge of interest in the technique of self-assessment under a property tax had its origin in some remarks made by Arnold C. Harberger at a conference (hereafter referred to as the Santiago Conference) concerned with Latin American tax problems. Amplification of the idea, additional discussion of it (both pro and con), and some variants of Harberger's proposal appear in the conference's proceedings and report. While the scheme initially was suggested for Latin American countries, or, more generally, countries who now have no property tax or only a rudimentary one, in fact, its potential advantages are not limited to such countries.[2] Any jurisdiction that levies on real property should be interested in a device that might achieve full value assessment and has been claimed to be simple and self-enforcing, to involve negligible costs, not to permit corruption, and to tend to push properties to their most productive use.

Self-Assessment: Design and Basic Requirements

Harberger has succinctly explained the rationale for self-assessment and proposed a particular version of the scheme as follows:

If taxes are to be levied, or income imputed, on the basis of the value of agricultural and/or residential properties, it is important that assessment procedures be adopted which estimate the true economic value of property with reasonable accuracy. Assessment procedures have been notably weak in most Latin American countires and are badly in need of reform. The economist's answer to the assessment problem is simple and essentially foolproof: allow each property owner to declare the value of his own property, make these declared values a matter of public record, and require that an owner sell his property to any bidder who is willing to pay say, 20 percent more than the declared value. This simple scheme is self-enforcing, allows no scope for corruption, has negligible costs of administration, and creates incentives, in addition to those already present in the market, for each property to be put to that use in which it has the highest economic productivity. The beauty of this scheme, so evident to economists, is not, however, appreciated by lawyers, who object strongly to the idea of requiring the sale of properties, possibly against the will of their owners. The economist can retort here that if owners value their property at the price at which they would be willing to sell, they should not be unwilling to sell at a price 20 percent higher.[3]

The essence of self-assessment, then, is that the owner of a property determines its value for tax purposes, that these values be made public, and that there be sanctions incorporated into the scheme that force such values to be realistic. The last is the nub of the matter. The *sine qua non* of successful self-assessment is a credible threat. Harberger's is a specific version of one type of sanction—the threat of forced sale. And he proposes that the owner be forced to sell to anybody who submits a legitimate bid. But, in principle, bidders could be limited to the government or to private persons or could include them both. For numerous reasons—the difficulty of valuing property with any precision, the need to prevent undue harassment, the possibility that particular properties may have a value to a particular owner in excess of its market value, etc.—it is desirable for public acceptance of self-assessment that the bid price that would force a sale be in excess of the owner's valuation. Harberger chose 20 percent as a reasonable figure in this connection.

Some other conference participants were opposed to Harberger's scheme for a number of reasons. Some argued against the principle of self-assessment, and others who supported the general principle proposed an alternative arrangement. Thus in the final report of the conference, a self-assessment scheme worthy of further consideration was described as follows:

. . . the declaration by the owner himself of the value of his property. This declaration would be placed on public record and any individual or enterprise would be free to make a bona fide bid to purchase the property. In the event that such a bid exceeded the owner's declared value by a significant amount (say, 20 percent), the owner, if he chose not to sell, would be required to revalue his property up to the amount which was bid. In this case, the maker of the frustrated bid would be entitled to a premium, which might be in the amount of the extra tax obtained in the first year following the revaluation of the property."[4]

And, as another variant, Nicholas Kaldor felt that self-assessment

. . . might be more acceptable if the owner always had the option of retaining his property if he revalued it above the offer made; for example, if an offer was made to buy the property at the owner's valuation plus 20 percent, the owner could retain it if he raised his valuation by 25 percent. That would lead to a correct valuation on the basis of a kind of auction, without involving forced sales. Mr. Harberger's original proposal might lead to certain difficulties; for example, an owner who was particularly attached to his property might overvalue it through fear of losing it, which would lead to resentment against the system.[5]

(While Kaldor does not note this specifically, presumably some reward would be provided for bidders whose offer was rebutted by the owner. Otherwise why would any bids be expected to be forthcoming?)

There are, then, at least three specific variants of a general self-assessment scheme. The first (for brevity we will call it the Harberger variant) requires that a self-assessed property be sold to anyone who submits a bona fide bid at least X percent greater than the owner's valuation. Harberger has specifically suggested an X of 20 percent. Another (which we will call the Conference Report variant) permits the owner to keep his property if he matches any bid at least Y percent greater than his valuation. Again a Y of 20 percent was suggested. The rebutted bidder would receive a reward, the specific amount suggested being the first year's increment in tax liability resulting from his bid.[6] Finally, Kaldor's variant permits the owner to keep his property in the face of a bid at least Z percent greater than his self-assessed value only if he declares a value of α percent greater than the self-assessed value, where $\alpha > Z$. Specifically, Kaldor suggested Z be 20 percent and α be 25 percent.[7] In the rest of our chapter, we will concentrate on two versions —Harberger's and the Conference Report's.

Whatever particular procedures are chosen, as stated above, the *sine qua non* of successful self-assessment is the credible threat.[8] For the system to work, underassessment must be costly to the property owner. He must be faced with a real and likely threat either of losing his property to the government or a higher private bidder or of paying a penalty if he chooses to retain his property after someone has submitted a bid on it.

It has sometimes been suggested that the government be relied on to keep self-assessment honest, simply by making the self-assessed valuation the basis for compensation in any land-taking for a public purpose—roads, slum clearance, public housing, urban renewal, purchases for land reserves, etc. It is doubtful that there is sufficient volume of such activity to constitute a credible threat. Government would, then, have to go out and make bids on underassessed properties or otherwise force their sale or cause the owner who underassessed to suffer some penalty.

Bids by government alone would probably be considered by

the public to be a less radical departure than the threat of forced sale to a private party (but it is still questionable whether it would be acceptable enough to pose no political danger for the government). Most governments have the right to appropriate land for good public reason. Unless government were simply to expropriate underassessed properties (a very unlikely possibility), reliance on public taking would limit the credible threat to the resources and the borrowing power of the government, and this would be considerably less than the financial capacity and acumen that the private sector and government together could muster. Moreover, even if there were no difference in financial resources, consideration of the limitations that "political realities" could put on government exercise of sanctions suggests that the threat of public taking would not push land use patterns toward optimality nor assessments upward to full value as strongly as would the threat of a private taking.

Permitting private party bids, on the other hand, would enlarge the fiscal capacity for the credible threat and self-assessment's push toward "best" land use (as noted above), but the legality of this procedure and its acceptability are more questionable. To lose one's property to a public institution is painful but perhaps bearable since it is somewhat similar to current practice. But to lose one's property to a private party might very well not be tolerated.

Very simply, then, a basic question posed for self-assessment is whether the community will "tolerate" it. To this we have no deft answer except to express our agreement with the judgment of others that the scheme would stand a better chance of acceptance if an alternative to forced sale were available. To ask whether the community will "tolerate" it is not to ask a loose or fuzzy question. Basically, we have in mind whether the people relied on to implement the credible threat—i.e., the bidders—will be permitted to function or whether they will be viewed and treated like informers or pariahs. It is not hard to think of a community's tacitly agreeing not to bid on each other's properties, in which case the threat would have to be implemented by "outsiders." Their bids would not be as knowledgeable as would, say, those of local real estate agents, nor would they have the support of local financial institutions.

However, if the community undertaking the experiment in self-assessment is "small," the fiscal resources of the rest of the country could be brought to bear on it. This, however, would lead to the most disagreeable of circumstances. "Outsiders" not wishing to live in "our" community would nonetheless be bidding on our properties. The fear of such a possibility could prevent the inception of self-assessment. Also, the fear of a boycott by the local people could deter outside bids if self-assessment were instituted. For who wants to bid on and acquire properties he cannot resell?

All this applies to forced sale. In a system where the owner had the option to revalue, public opposition would not be as strong, but it would by no means be mild. Witness the experience with tax ferrets.[9]

Assume, however, that this hurdle has been passed and the community has decided to introduce self-assessment. Will it in fact have the fiscal and administrative capacity to implement the credible threat? In part the answer may depend importantly on what version is chosen, but something can be said in a general way also.

There is, of course, no basis for determining precisely how big a job implementing a credible threat would be. It is conceivable that simply stern talk and an appearance of readiness would induce substantially full value self-assessments. A more likely initial result, however, is that some people will stand ready to test the system of sanctions. How many there would be is hard to say. But, even with a relatively modest fraction of properties requiring sanctions, the strain on financial and marketing resources could become prohibitive. Illustrative a priori (but seemingly reasonable) figures might help point up this difficulty. Suppose one in four properties is understated sufficiently so that "takeover" bids are in order and a one-fifth likelihood of being bid on is needed to make the threat effective. Therefore, people will have to bid on and stand ready to purchase one-twentieth of all properties. If on the average, however, only 10 percent of property turns over every year,[10] then property transfers will have to increase by 50 percent. And this increase, in turn, would require a very substantial increase in the energy devoted to property exchanges and in the administrative facilities and the finance needed to effectuate them. For many municipalities, it is doubtful if local financial institutions and entrepreneurs could support such an endeavor. This is not to suggest that the increase in market functionaries and required finances would be precisely 50 percent. It is entirely possible, first, that a high proportion of the underassessed properties would have been in the 10 percent that would have been sold anyway; secondly, that mechanisms might be developed to allow more efficient utilization of existing property marketing institutions (such as professional arbitrageurs); and, finally, that the government might develop a program of loan insurance that would permit banks to make loans with smaller down payments. So the strength of our objection here is an empirical question. Nonetheless, a heavy and perhaps unbearable strain on existing facilities is a real possibility as a concomitant of the credible threat requirement. Again, with owners permitted the option to revalue and few properties actually taken over, the problem of fiscal capacity does not loom as large.

An objection to the Harberger form of self-assessment that has worried lawyers particularly is the constitutional problem of forced private sale. Basically, it appears questionable whether anyone can be forced to sell his property to another private party, even when the price is reasonable. The state, it is generally recognized, has the right to force property to be sold to it for the benefit of the community, but a private person does not have the right to force a sale for his own benefit (even if in the process he is tangentially benefiting the community via higher taxes, etc.). Legal competence is required for full discussion of this issue, but the nonspecialist can sense that this will be a very delicate as well as emotional problem. If forced sale to a private party is unconstitutional, however, many of the alleged benefits of self-assessment ("simple," "self-enforcing") would not materialize and the burden of enforcement would be entirely on the government or on bidders, to be rewarded by bonuses out of the increased taxes engendered by their bids which forced owners to revalue or by fines levied on underassessors. We will argue below that this is likely to be less effective than forced sale.

Enforcement, then, which is the heart of the self-assessment proposal, may not be as simple or as automatic as it might seem at first glance. And complicating the problem of enforcement is the hazard that communities that enforce self-assessment vigorously may lose resources and activities to places that are more lax. This point, of course, is not unique to self-assessment; it is relevant to any tax measure. More particular to self-assessment, however, is the real danger that differential severity of enforcement among cities could result from their differential capacity to mount a credible threat.

The ability to undertake bids, i.e., to profit from underassessment, would also differ, of course, among the individuals in the community. The rich, having financial resources to make their bids bona fide, are more able to bid than the poor. This situation would be strengthened by the greater ability to borrow of those who already have resources. Moreover, those who are knowledgeable about property would be in a position to benefit to a greater extent than those who are not. Suppose the whole community started out the self-assessment experiment with substantial underassessment. In the process of bidding up to full value assessment, the rich and knowledgeable would benefit at the expense of the poor and uninformed. This is hardly a result that is likely to endear self-assessment to the majority of taxpayers.

Conceivably, self-assessment could lead to a higher cost of administration, not the lower one that has been claimed for it, if property owners, ignorant of the real value of their properties, turn to professional appraisers for advice on a large scale, if bidders also appraise property as they must, and if government is called on to make appraisals, too, when owners appeal.

Moreover, considerable resentment might be generated by the exposure of property owners to any kind of irrational bid. It is not sufficient to answer that it should be consolation enough for the owner to receive a payment that is 20 percent more than he considers the property to be worth. Owners may not wish this bonus. It is of the nature of property rights that an owner can sell or *not* sell. In this sense forced sale would constitute a fundamental change in the structure of property rights. This could be considered too high a price to pay for better administration of the tax. The Conference Report variant, while it would still permit an owner to stave off an irrational bid by matching it, would, nonetheless, require him to pay a tax penalty for the privilege. This, too, could arouse resentment.

Nor is it difficult to think of a variety of dodges that ingenious property owners might resort to in order to minimize their assessments or otherwise beat the system. Two owners of similar properties might sell them to each other for, say, one dollar, and lease them back for ninety-nine years at a dollar a year. To any bidder a property so encumbered is worthless; thus the owners could put a low value on them for tax purposes. Or, as another example, under the revaluation option, owners who had been forced up to market price by excessive bids could drop back to any level they wanted the next year, and many would do this as long as it was only the government's revenue they were playing with. If, in addition to paying higher taxes, they also had to pay a fine, there would be less incentive to jockey self-assessments. Yet the pressure would always be present.

Earlier we mentioned the lack of protection from "irrational" offers. This could be more broadly conceived to cover all cases of "uneconomic" decisions in which people are willing to pay more than the market price or to accept less. On such decisions self-assessment with either forced sale or the rebidding option would have two contradictory influences. (As noted earlier, the pressures would, in general, be less severe when the owner could frustrate the bid.) Self-assessment, as its proponents claim, would make "uneconomic" action more costly by requiring people who engage in it to pay higher taxes. But it would also, as its critics point out, facilitate "uneconomic" action in the sense that a property is made available to anyone who wishes to pay enough for it. Thus under self-assessment, whites who were insisting on prices that would keep Negroes out of a neighborhood would be required to pay higher taxes as the penalty for their noneconomic reservation prices. And, on the other hand, those whites who were willing to pay such a penalty could make very high bids, thus using the system of self-assessment to make it prohibitively costly for Negroes who had moved into a predominantly white neighborhood to stay there. Clearly, in the latter case, the law would have to incorporate relief procedures that would try to prevent this kind of abuse of the system. But administrative complexities and litigation can be expected when the motive for and reasonableness of an offer have to be inquired into. And undoubtedly it would be impossible to prevent all harassment.

This is by no means a complete list of the problems that might bedevil and indeed disable self-assessment of property values under a property tax. But it is sufficient to indicate that whether such a system could ever get off the ground is an open question. We have no strong convictions about it, and we do not think that these difficulties summarily rule out further consideration of self-assessment. So we leave this as an open question and go on to examine what kinds of valuations might be expected from a system of self-assessment.

The Results of Self-Assessment

In essence self-assessment with enforcing sanctions can be viewed as an auction or series of auctions. The primary questions that need to be answered in evaluating the process are how rapid and thorough is the auction, and how equitable are its results?

We have just seen that there may be good reason to think that a more basic question is in order, viz., "Can the auction be held at all?" But since we decided to leave that open, let us examine what might happen to a self-assessment scheme (herein abbreviated to S.A.) with forced sale (F.S.) or with an option for the owner to match (O.M.) and thus frustrate the bid. Our discussion starts with the simplest and least realistic case and proceeds by relaxing assumptions and introducing other considerations to examine the set of property values that might be expected from S.A. with F.S. or O.M. While the discussion will be quite general, it will be convenient at some points to refer to a specific set of numbers, in which case we will use the Harberger proposal for F.S. and the Conference Report proposal for O.M.

Certainty

Let $V = $ "true" value of the property, $A = $ self-assessed value, and $X = $ fractional premium required for a bona fide bid with either F.S. or O.M.

Assume that (1) the values of all properties are known (and are one and the same value) to everyone in the community; (2) owners are satisfied with their property holdings (i.e., they do not wish to part with them at less than V) ; and (3) there is in fact enough fiscal capacity and a large enough supply of entrepreneurial bidding zeal to insure that every property's true value can be captured; moreover, everyone knows this is so.

With these assumptions, under F.S. the owner, to protect his property, will assess at $V/(1 + X)$, which is just high enough to prevent a takeover bid, since the latter would have to be at $(1 + X)(V)/(1 + X)$, which would leave no profit for the takeover. Should the owner value his property at less than $V/(1 + X)$, he will lose it; whereas it is unnecessary for him to value it at anything greater than $V/(1 + X)$ to keep it. Under O.M. (which specifically, we assume, also requires that a bid exceed the owner's valuation by X, with the premium for a frustrated bid being one year's increase in tax liability because of the owner's matching of the bid) it might seem that the owner able to revalue his property without any penalty other than increased taxes and desiring to postpone paying his fair share of the tax as long as possible would value his property initially at zero (or enough above zero to keep him less conspicuous than the other undervaluers). But, under our assumption, bids will be forthcoming at V from bidders who wish to maximize the value of their premium. The owner would then frustrate the bid and end up with a property assessed at V for tax purposes. However, by immediately assessing his property at $V/(1 + X)$, he could insure a lower tax basis for it. We conclude, then, that with the assumptions set out above (which among other things mean that the bidder has no chance of a capital gain and can only seek a bounty on a frustrated bid), under either F.S. or O.M., the property valuation process and its results will be the same, viz., instantaneous setting by the owners of $V/(1 + X)$ as the value of properties. If, for example, $X = \frac{1}{5}$, properties will be valued by their owners at $(\frac{5}{6})$ V.

The goal of full value assessment will not have been achieved. Indeed, providing that the bid must exceed the owner's assessment by any X assures this. Yet, the failure to achieve full value assessment seems of little real significance. With all properties the same proportion of their "true" value, a given total tax liability will be distributed among them just as it would be had they all been assessed at 100 percent.

Taking Account of Doubt that Self-Assessment will be Completely Enforced

If assumption (3) above is relaxed and there exists some skepticism about the capacity or desire to implement the credible threat, then, in effect, owners should think of gambling. Optimistically, they could underassess without penalty. But even were they to be bid on, it might be later rather than sooner. In theory, then, owners might value their properties as low as zero, but, more realistically, they would set a value somewhere in the range bounded by a lower value sufficiently above zero to keep them from being conspicuous and by an upper value equal to $V/(1 + X)$.

How close ultimate valuations (or, more realistically, valuations after some reasonable time) would come to the upper bound—$V/(1 + X)$—would depend on how adequate fiscal capacity and the supply of bidding talent were. With the penalty for undervaluation more severe for F.S. than for O.M., self-assessments under the former would initially be higher than under the latter. (Remember, the penalty with F.S. is loss of one's property at less than the market price, while under

O.M., if adoption of the Conference Report proposal is assumed, the penalty is simply an increased tax liability.) Moreover, with the capital gains to bidders in a scheme that relied on F.S. being larger than the premiums to frustrated bidders under O.M., more bids would be forthcoming under F.S. On these two scores, then, owners' valuations would most likely be higher initially and at any point in time under F.S. than under O.M. On other grounds, it is plausible, *ceteris paribus,* to expect more bids under O.M., because, with bids frustrated, less financial capacity would be needed to bring underassessed properties up. However, on net balance, we think our judgment about the relative strengths of F.S. and O.M. still applies.

Finally, an additional disadvantage of O.M. (at least in the version proposed for consideration by the Santiago Conference) arises from the fact that the bounty for bidding is supported out of what would otherwise be the government's tax revenue. Property owners, in effect, are gambling with the government's tax revenue at no cost to themselves. So for the tax authority, the results under S.A. with O.M. would be less attractive than with F.S. for two reasons: O.M. would probably have a lower level of assessments; and under the Conference Report proposal, increments in tax revenue associated with frustrated bids would, in the first instance, go to the bidders. Under F.S., however, the system of rewards and penalties is entirely privately financed; the capital losses of owners who have to surrender their properties are the counterpart of the capital gains, the expectation of which elicits bids on the property.

These differences between F.S. and O.M. rest, of course, on our judgment of the relative strengths of the two schemes, and, in particular, our estimates of the volume of bidding that would be required and the amount of bidding that would be forthcoming under each of them. Some students have argued that to make a series of bids that are likely to be frustrated is a substantially different process—both speedier and requiring less in the way of fiscal resources—than bidding in the expectation that a real property transfer will take place. We acknowledged this above, but expressed the judgment that for other reasons F.S. would be more effective than O.M. This is what we think, but it is only fair to add that we have no firm basis for this judgment.

Moreover, the difference between the results under F.S. and those under O.M. is strongly dependent on the particular version of each of the schemes that we have chosen to compare. The Conference Report suggestion embodies no real penalty against the underassessor. He can retain his property merely by raising his valuation to that placed on it by the bidder. Under such conditions, it pays, of course, to defer this "day of judgment" as long as possible. In theory, the government could rectify this situation by providing that the increased payment due from the owner in order for him to retain his property in the face of a takeover bid would be the compounded value of all taxes deferred from self-assessing at less than the takeover bid value. This would require determining how long the property had been underassessed, calculating a new tax bill for each year it was in this state, and compounding these taxes to the present. This procedure would, of course, serve to deter underassessment (but not to obliterate it; it still pays to gamble because you may not be detected). But it would also be complex enough to eliminate the simplicity that is claimed as one of the strong appeals of self-assessment.

The government, of course, need not stop at this. It could, if it wished, make the penalty for underassessing arbitrarily severe, say, five or ten times the annual increase in the owner's tax liability caused by his matching a takeover bid. While it might seem that the threat of compulsory sale is a more severe sanction than the payment of a fine, in fact it depends on how severe the fine might be. A heavy enough fine could discourage underassessment more strongly than the possibility of compulsory sale. But such a fine might seem so "inhuman" as to discourage adoption of self-assessment. However, the specific fines that have been proposed do not come close to this. Indeed, they do not appear to be strong deterrents. For example, Strasma (see citation in note 2) suggests that, to retain his property once a bid has been made, the owner must pay the additional tax liability due that year and a fine equal to twice the additional amount as well. As an illustration, this plan would require that, under a 3 percent tax rate, the owner of the house he assessed at $15,000 would, in the face of a bid of $25,000, have to pay $300 more in taxes for that year and a fine of $600 as well. The fine apparently would be invariant with respect to the period during which the property was underassessed; on this score, the fine would not constitute so severe a deterrent to playing the underassessment game. Moreover, $600 seems small in comparison with the amount that someone who now owns a property worth $25,000 would pay not to have to give it up. The transaction costs and inconvenience in connection with acquiring an equally valuable property, to say nothing of consumer surplus (which is taken up at some length below), should come to considerably more than $600. So a two-year fine does not appear to be heavy enough to have the same bite as forced sale. If, say, the 20 percent premium suggested by Harberger is a reasonable upper bound on measures of the value of not having to sell a property and find another one, the upper bound on the set of fines suitable to the numbers of our illustration would be more on the order of seventeen times the annual increase in tax liability.[11]

Fines, however, could help serve another purpose. They could help support a higher level of premium to the frustrated bidder, and thereby would be instrumental in eliciting more bidding activity. The heavier the premium frustrated bidders can expect, the more bidding there will be. The merit of a system of fines from the tax authority's point of view is that they could support heavy premiums to frustrated bidders, which otherwise could be provided, in effect, only at the expense of additional tax revenue. Thus Strasma (again see note 2) proposes that half the sum of the change in annual tax payment, plus the fine (i.e., twice the change in annual tax payment), be awarded the maker of a frustrated bid. This boils down to a payment to the bidder equal to 150 percent of the increase in tax liability resulting from his bid, which, of course, is more generous than the Conference Report's proposal of one year's change in tax liability.

It is axiomatic that larger premiums will encourage more bidding. But how large a premium must be provided to induce sufficient bidding to make effective a system of self-assessment in which the property holder has the option of frustrating a bid? We do not know how to answer this question, but can suggest some of the considerations relevant to an answer. Bidding, like any other economic activity, must provide a return similar to that obtainable in alternative lines of effort, after due allowance for their relative risk. Whatever system of self-assessment is used, bids must be bona fide; there must be a willingness and capacity to purchase the property. The capacity is the bidder's capital, and how much he earns a year on it depends on how frequently he turns it over. If, to be bona fide, a bid must be backed by financial capacity equal to 25 percent of its amount, if the typical biddable property is, like our illustrative example, worth $25,000 and is self-assessed at $15,000, if the premium to the frustrated bidder is one year's change in tax liability, as the Conference Report proposed, and if the making of a bid and its frustration are consummated within a week, then bidding would be a very profitable occupation. For an annual investment of $6,250 would return $15,000 per year. (For arithmetic simplicity, we assume bidders take a vacation of two weeks each year.) If, however, everything else being the same, the period of consummation is more like six months, then bidding would be a fairly unattractive occupation, especially with the risks associated with it—one of them being the risk of becoming a pariah. Needless to say, this so-called conclusion is arbitrary, resting as it does solely on the particular numbers chosen. Such numbers can be generated without limit, and in Table 6.1 we have reproduced some. Most of the cells in the table show frustrated bidding to be a good business to get into. But what the real facts are likely to be, we do not know.

In concluding this section, we note that it contains no discussion of the Kaldor variant outlined above. In principle his scheme falls somewhere between the Harberger and the Conference Report proposals, lying closer to the latter, and does not seem to require special discussion.

TABLE 6.1

ANNUAL RATE OF RETURN (PERCENT) ON INVESTMENT IN FRUSTRATED BIDS*

| | Self-assessed value as fraction of "true" value | | | | | | | |
| | .2 | | .4 | | .6 | | .8 | |
Bid consummation period	a	b	a	b	a	b	a	b
1 week (50 times per year)	480	240	360	180	240	120	120	60
1 month	115	58	86	43	58	29	29	14
3 months	38	19	29	14	19	10	10	5
6 months	19	10	14	7	10	5	5	2
1 year	10	5	7	4	5	2	2	1

* Assumes an effective property tax rate of 3 percent.
a = 25 percent down payment for bona fide bid.
b = 50 percent down payment for bona fide bid.

Relaxing the Assumption of Perfect Knowledge

In setting out to discuss what set of valuations might be expected under self-assessment, we assumed that all property values were known to and agreed on by everyone in the community. There are, of course, numerous grounds for questioning the realism of this assumption. Two, in particular, are worth further examination.

For one thing, property owners are "amateurs" and bidders would be "professionals." In the normal course of events, professionals should be expected to know more than amateurs.

For another, the satisfied holder of a property will consider it to be worth *at least* its market value, whereas bidders who are in business for a capital gain under F.S. (or a premium or capital gain under O.M.) will consider the property to be worth *no more* than its market value. The difference between their two appraisals of the same property could be important.

We will consider each of these bases for relaxing the assumption of perfect knowledge in turn and at some length.

"Amateurs" and "professionals."—A simple way of relaxing the universal perfect knowledge assumption is to exaggerate the difference between owners and bidders by assuming that owners' valuations are a random variable, $\tilde{V}$, and any particular self-assessment of the property, A, will fall within a range

indicated by this random process, whereas bidders know precisely the value for each property, say, V^*. Owners, then, would see their properties as having values that fall in a range that extends above and below V^*. Were there no "mark-up" over the owner's valuation required for a bid to be bona fide (i.e., were there no X requirement), whenever owners set A at less than V^*, bidders would take over the property by offering just a little more than A for it, while whenever the owner's assessed value was above the true value, no bids would be forthcoming, and owners would keep the property. The net result would be that owners would keep overvalued properties, while bidders would obtain undervalued properties. The aggregate of tax liabilities would remain the same (if need be government would adjust rates commensurately to raise the given amount of revenue it requires), but it would be distributed more heavily on properties kept by owners and less heavily on properties taken over by bidders than before. In addition there would have been a transfer of wealth from erstwhile owners to successful bidders. Under these more realistic assumptions, self-assessment would appear to have distributional effects unfavorable to owners. How serious these would be, we cannot, of course, state a priori. Over time, however, this initial position would be modified. If bidders sell the properties they acquired at V^* (in other words we are assuming the erstwhile owners "learn" about true values), they will enjoy a capital gain and the properties will be valued "correctly" for tax purposes; while owners who kept their properties will "learn" from finding no bids submitted on them and will tend to put lower assessments on them. Thus market valuation of property would be approached. The pace of this process and how closely assessments would approach V^* would depend on the fiscal capacity and entrepreneurial energy available for bidding.

But, in fact, in the scheme of F.S. under discussion, bids are bona fide and must be taken only if they exceed the owner's A by X. So only those properties underassessed by owners sufficiently that $(1 + X)A < V^*$ will be bid on. Properties whose values are such that $(1 + X)A > V^*$ will be immunized from bidding. Again, under the assumption that owners "learn" about V^*, the properties that bidders have taken over will be sold, and the new owners, to protect them, need assess at no more than $V^*/(1 + X)$. Also, owners whose assessments are higher than this, finding themselves untroubled by bids, will tend to lower their assessments back to $V^*/(1 + X)$. Once more the speed of this approach and how far it goes will be determined by how strongly the threat of forced sale can be implemented. As reasoned above, until the adjustment is completed, the property tax burden will have been shifted to bear more heavily on owners who have retained their properties, while those who have had to give them up will have suffered capital losses. The higher X, the less will be the capital losses suffered by property owners. The converse, of course, is this: the higher X, the lower the "equilibrium" level of property assessments, i.e., the lower $V^*/(1 + X)$. It is worth noting again that a singular result of any self-assessment scheme with the requirement that the bid exceed the owner's assessment by some finite amount is that it will never achieve full value assessments for all properties. Yet this shortfall is really important only insofar as it affects the distribution of property tax liability. Under our first set of simple assumptions (and here, also, by virtue of our failing to specify much about the process that generates $\tilde{V}$), we had self-assessments predictably below full market value to the same percentage for each and every property in the "steady state"; hence, no change in the distribution would be expected. As we will argue below, however, there are good grounds in more realistic cases for expecting a differential result among properties, and, therefore, a change in relative tax burdens.

It is worth noting, too, that under our assumption of unequal knowledge, initial owners will be disadvantaged, some as regards tax liability and others in respect to capital losses. This might be considered the penalty they pay for relative ignorance or the price they pay to learn, i.e., their "tuition fee."

How many such properties, i.e., properties self-assessed by their owners at less than $V^*/(1 + X)$, are there likely to be? The few data we have indicate that, under our assumptions, the number could be surprisingly large. To explain this judgment requires a fairly long excursion, which we justify not simply for its help in generating this number but because it is evidence more generally germane to the evaluation of a self-assessment scheme.

A major objection to all assessment schemes, but, in our judgment, more particularly to self-assessment, lies in the great difficulty of determining the "true" value of real estate. So difficult is this valuation that it is entirely possible that, for a good many properties, professionals would have to be employed at a cost greater than or equal to the cost of government assessment. Thus, the administrative advantage of self-assessment would be spurious, for it would merely involve shifting costs from government to individuals.

The scattered evidence we have suggests another difficulty. The goal of accurate assessment, while noble, may not be feasible. Our property tax assessment experience gives little comfort; it indicates that even trained professionals differ substantially in their assessment of property values. As summarized in a note in the *Harvard Law Review:*

> The [Census] Bureau studied 1,263 localities throughout the country and found that the degree of assessment equality accepted by most experts as a reasonable and obtainable goal had been achieved in only one-fifth of them. This conclusion is amply supported by reported cases and other evidence of current assessment practices. In a recent South Dakota case the trial court found that property of the *same class* had been assessed at rates ranging from 13.3 to 131 percent of the value. The Wichita, Kansas, Chamber of Commerce reports that in five bona fide sales of downtown office buildings within the past two years the ratio of assessed to market value were respectively 26, 41, 43, 46, and 65 percent. . . . And the New Jersey Supreme Court was confronted last year with findings that assessment ratios within a given municipality for the year in question ranged from 4.13 to 86 percent on vacant lands, and from 5.13 to 79.88 percent on other properties.[12]

Among the most thorough of the recent studies in this field is one by Oldman and Aaron, who examined the pattern of differentials in property assessment in a particular case, Boston.[13] They found as follows:

1. A systematic difference exists among assessment-sales ra-

tios on classes of property. The ratio averaged 34 percent in the case of single-family residences, 42 percent for two-family dwellings, 52 percent for three- to five-family houses, 58 percent for residences housing six or more families, and 79 percent for commercial property.

2. There are patterns of inequalities associated with price within each category of property. Thus "for most classes of residential property the average ratio declined for each successively higher class," but "the patterns are not smooth."

3. For any given class of property the assessment-sales ratio had a sizable standard deviation, and, as among different classes of property, there were wide variations in the standard deviation of the ratio. Specifically, they report for various property categories the following standard deviations of assessment-sales ratios.

Single family	.150
Two families or apartments	.195
Three to five familes or apartments	.274
Six or more families or apartments	.206
Commercial	.411
Land	.439

(In a preliminary draft, Oldman and Aaron warned that they had so few observations on vacant land that "it would be hazardous to make generalizations about this category." Yet, pointing to its high standard deviation, they noted specifically "the problem that this would create for any assessment scheme —especially one with forced sale provisions.")

All this adds up to a well-documented picture of stark differences in assessed value relative to market value; for these differences there seem to be two underlying causes—purposeful policy and random errors of measurement. The systematic patterns noted under (1) and also, perhaps, (2) above can, as a first approximation, be taken to be the result of a purposeful policy to bring assessments closer to "true" value on some classes of properties than on others. Assume that, in the absence of this policy, the assessment-sales ratio for all classes of property would average unity. The standard deviations noted in (3) above, however, which, as a first approximation, can be taken to be the result of random errors of measurement, indicate that the observed assessment-sales ratios will be widely dispersed around their expected value of one. And it is this latter evidence, as Oldman and Aaron note, that is particularly germane to an evaluation of self-assessment. These data direct attention to the inherent difficulties of property valuation that suggest special problems for self-assessment.

To put the point directly, under self-assessment with forced sale a legitimate "mistake" could mean the loss of one's property. Since the large standard deviations suggest that mistakes are quite likely, it would seem that S.A. with F.S. could bring many hard cases, i.e., cases of unwitting forced sale.

Illustrating with the Oldman-Aaron data, let us assume that the purposeful errors that account for an assessment-sales ratio of less than one (i.e., that incorporate policy decisions to assess some classes of properties more heavily than others) are eliminated by self-assessment, but that the randomness remains, and that the process of property assessment can be described as a normally distributed random variable with an expected assessment-sales ratio of one and the standard deviation, σ, as measured by Oldman-Aaron. Assume further that the data as measured for assessments in Boston by Oldman and Aaron characterize the owners' valuation process. (Since their data come from assessments made by professional assessors, that is, in fact, an optimistic assumption for property owners, who are amateurs. We could make the assumption "realistic" by assuming, additionally, that owners hire professional assessors to make their valuations. And we could also lend realism to the assumption that "professionals" always are able to assign a value of V^*—the mean of the values in the process that generates the random variable $\tilde{V}$—by the further assumption that a large team of assessors works for the bidding syndicate and each member of the team assesses each property, with the syndicate operating under the rule that it always bids the mean of these assessments.) Then for two-family residential properties, say, whose σ was .195, we know that slightly less than one-sixth of all two-family homes would have an assessment-sales ratio of less than 0.8.[14] If the sale price is assumed to be the market value, these homes would have been valued at less than 80 percent of their market value. If, as has been suggested, the self-assessment system would not permit takeover bids unless they exceeded the owner's assessment by, say, 20 percent, this group of homes would be biddable. This example also suggests incidentally the strong need for a sizable premium of bid price over self-assessed price, for otherwise the number of bids required would be extremely large.

Thus, although owners individually valued as accurately as Boston assessors, one-sixth of all two-family homes would have values set by owners that would be far enough below market value to be an attractive target for a takeover bid *even in the face of a condition that such bids must exceed the owner's assessment by 20 percent*. *Per se* this is not a criticism of self-assessment, since by our assumption the "error" here is just as great as that in regular assessment. But the consequences would seem to be more severe. For, even though in regular assessment the errors are as pronounced, they result only in overtaxation or undertaxation, whereas under self-assessment the consequences could be forced sale or fine. But is there really any "hardship" here? Won't these victims "cry all the way to the bank"? If forced to sell, these homeowners would receive a price considerably more than they thought their homes were worth. Yet this, too, is not all of the story, for with the proceeds of the sale they could not in general replace the properties they were forced to sell. It also seems clear that a system of assessment and associated enforcement that puts, say, one-sixth of well-intentioned homeowners who have been honest in their valuations in the position of having to part with their home upon a bid from a more "knowledgeable" party, is not likely to be strongly supported or perhaps even tolerated by the community, even though there would be monetary assuagement should the homes be bid away.[15] We take this to be a serious disability of self-assessment.

The specific numbers of the Boston experience are not the heart of the matter, and have been used only to illustrate the problem. Had we referred to single-family houses—for which the standard deviation was .15—the problem would not have seemed as severe, although it would not, of course, be inconsequential. And notice, on the other hand, how much stronger a case for our conclusion could have been made had we used vacant land, for which the standard deviation was .44, to illustrate the point. In fact, this case would have been too good, for it would have a sizable number of observations with negative assessment-sales ratios, an impossibility since it requires that either the assessed or the sales value be negative; that, in turn, would direct critical attention to our simplifying assumptions that the assessment-sales ratio is a normally distributed random variable. Despite the looseness of the assumptions, however, we think the point is valid. Moreover, the real estate valuation process probably has smaller variances in a community with well-developed and active real estate markets—Boston —than in many smaller cities. Thus our illustrative figures understate the seriousness of this problem for some other communities.

Finally, in closing this subsection, we undertake no extended discussion of O.M. and its comparison with F.S., because it would be substantially the same as that in earlier sections, with the exception that the observations on the potential harshness of self-assessment on some well-intentioned property owners strictly apply only to forced sale.

"Consumers surplus."—Our initial assumption that values are agreed on and known to all can be relaxed in another way, i.e., by a recognition of the possible divergence in assessment of the worth of a commodity between those who hold it for consumption and those who wish to purchase it, but only for resale. The point we shall develop here has been noted earlier in our chapter and was, in fact, made by several of the participants at the Santiago Conference. Indeed, it is one of the reasons given by supporters of S.A. with F.S. for the requirement that, to be considered bona fide, a bid must exceed the owner's assessment by some specified percentage. But here we wish to explore the matter at somewhat greater length.

We start by observing that homes serve a multiplicity of needs, all of which influence the purchase decision. In a very real sense they are highly differentiated commodities providing not only shelter but access to work, shopping, schooling and recreation, neighborhood friendships and activities, closeness to relatives, etc. Thus for some homeowners, and it could be that they are many, there may not, in fact, be a large number of substitutes available at the market price that will provide the same set of services (or an equally satisfactory combination of qualities) as their present house. These homeowners, then, would be not at all sanguine about the prospects of getting as satisfactory a housing situation as they now have should they have to sell their house at the current market price and buy another with the proceeds.

It is not a distinction of homeowners that, for all but the marginal owner, a house is worth more than its market price. With every asset all but the marginal holders would have been willing in fact to pay more than the market price for it. So it is not "consumers surplus" *per se* that we are discussing. Rather it is the relative scarcity of good substitutes that seems to be the main difference. To focus the point, we think that there is a distinction between homes and, say, cars in this connection. Car owners would experience less distress than homeowners if forced to give up their asset at market price, because the payment would come closer to permitting the purchase of an equally satisfactory replacement for a car than for a home. (Remember we are reckoning in here the transaction costs, the costs of search, and items or utilities that are not purchasable or reimbursable, e.g., "the best home in the neighborhood," etc.)

Given, then, the relative lack of equally satisfying housing alternatives at a given price, homeowners under a self-assessment scheme would seek to protect their "extra value." That is to say, even if they knew the market value with precision, they would, except for the marginal owner, set a value that incorporates some part at least of the excess of what the house is worth to them over what they would have to pay for it in the market were it freely for sale. Some part, at least, of "consumers surplus" in this sense would appear in their assessments. Let us turn back to automobiles for a moment: if automobiles were to be self-assessed for tax purposes, we would expect the values set by taxpayers to aggregate to just about as much as their market value. For homes, we would expect the self-assessed values to come to more than the market value of the housing stock. However, it is possible simply to argue that incorporation of "consumers surplus" in the valuation base is not bad in itself. It merely means the tax base will be higher; and if a specified amount of revenue is to be raised, tax rates will be commensurately lower.

But this dismisses the problem too glibly. The degree of incorporation of "consumers surplus" in assessed value will not be uniform for all taxpayers, nor will the amount of "consumers surplus" be the same for all. Besides one's taste for housing, the extent to which "consumers surplus" is incorporated will be determined by the homeowner's degree of risk aversion as well as his ability to undertake and support a search for alternatives.

Since, at any given level of value of housing ownership, the degree of risk aversion varies with owners' tastes, a horizontal inequity would develop. *De facto* rates of tax would be higher for properties of equal value the greater the degree of the taxpayer's aversion to risk. Moreover, one might argue that a reasonable property of utility functions is that risk aversion decreases with increasing income.[16] (Certainly the rich, *ceteris paribus*, have a greater capacity to assume risk.) Under these conditions, self-assessment would tend to discriminate against homeowners on the basis of income. And this vertical inequity too could be a serious objection to self-assessment.

Knowledge of alternatives is unevenly distributed among the population (with people in some professions such as real estate and banking, obviously, being more knowledgeable than others), as is the capacity to undertake search and support it. But these latter abilities are probably correlated with wealth. There does not seem to be too much to say, a priori, about whether the "poor" or the "rich" would be able more easily to find housing equally satisfactory to their present premises at the respective going market price. On the one hand, the homes of the rich are more individual in design and location, but, on the other, the poor are more limited in their locational options because of low incomes and because the journey to work may be an important consideration.

In sum, then, there are good grounds for believing that under self-assessment, divergent assessments would be made by the owners of properties of similar market value. And these differentials would reflect not only the amount of "consumers surplus" but also the owners' taste for risks, their income, knowledge of alternatives, and wealth. A system of property taxation which, when the self-assessment rolls were opened to inspection, showed a wide variation in the assessed values of homes that have the same market value could not be expected to command public support or appear to be a real improvement over administered assessment.

Ironically, then, one can argue that self-assessment would provide a tax base that is too subtle insofar as elements of "consumers surplus" are brought into it. This is a degree of sophistication not currently achieved by our most highly developed tax—the federal government's levy on personal income. For purposes of that tax the base is the dollar amount of income, not the capacity for enjoyment that it means for the taxpayer. Calibration among taxpayers is according to an objective monetary amount. Under self-assessment with forced sale (but still for this moment no premium on the takeover bid), a likely result will be a tax base for each homeowner that is somewhere between what he can sell his house for and what he would pay not to have to give up that house. Thus one could expect self-assessment to lead to a set of varying divergences between true and assessed values.

The introduction of elements of utility into the tax base we consider a criticism of self-assessment because it departs from the practice for other taxes. However, it would mean a more subtle base, and in this sense, one could argue it is an advantage. Yet we are impressed with the differential feature of the problem. Utility would be brought in, but to different degrees depending on the taxpayer's ability and willingness to bear risk, his knowledge of alternatives and his ability to search for them, his ability to move, etc.

Parenthetically and by way of formal correctness we observe that, while the major implications have already been wrung out of the "consumers surplus" argument, we have stated it as if homeowners' valuations will run from V^* and up, whereas they would be from $V^* / (1 + X)$ up. Aside from this, everything holds as argued.

Some other possibilities.—Our discussion of the set of valuations that might result from self-assessment has really merely scratched the surface of a group of very complex problems. This fact does not necessarily mean that the conclusions we have reached are invalid. It does, however, suggest that they should be reviewed as "tendencies" or "likelihoods," rather than predictions of what, in fact, would happen.

At a number of points in the discussion we explored what might eventuate were a particular assumption to apply. We have neither the time nor the ingenuity to examine all possible alternative assumptions, but in this section we do consider a few.

Above, in relaxing the perfect knowledge assumption, we had the owners' valuations be a random variable, but kept bidders perfectly knowledgeable. But suppose both owners' and bidders' property valuations are a random variable; what then?

Start by assuming property valuation to be, say, a random normal process with a mean assessment-sales ratio of one. Under such conditions, after all the properties in a jurisdiction have been assessed by the usual process, half of them will be undervalued and half overvalued. Now let there be, as there would be in a self-assessment scheme, two sets of valuers, each characterized by the same random process, and let them assess each property simultaneously. Each "assessor," then, can value every property either too high or too low with probability one-half. Call the two sets of assessors, one apiece for each property, owners and bidders. Owners can set either too high or too low a value (the probability of a particular event—say, "setting just the right value"—being zero in a continuous distribution), as can bidders.

We neglect the premium required on a takeover bid, for the

moment. For each property, since the higher value keeps it or gets it, the probability that it will be overvalued will be one minus the probability that both owners and bidders undervalue. Since these are independent valuations, the probability that both owners and bidders undervalue is .25, and the probability that a property will be overvalued is .75. This contrasts with the results of the usual assessment procedures, by which only half the properties would be overvalued. But this may not be a severe indictment of self-assessment. For, if, as we assumed, this process of valuation is random, independent, and symmetrical with respect to owners and bidders, each will have equal proportions of overvalued and undervalued properties, so there will have been no redistribution of total tax base as between the two groups. And since government's goal is a given tax revenue, rates will simply be lower in the face of higher assessments. Moreover, with enough of these annual valuation lotteries, each property will tend to have an average assessment equal to its true value.

Of course, in any real self-assessment arrangement, properties will not change hands at the dizzying rate just stated, nor would there be so great a degree of overvaluation. Also, any legitimate bid would have to be at least $(1 + X)$ greater than the owner's valuation. So there would be fewer exchanges and a lesser degree of overvaluation.

This illustration is not completely empty, however. We can use it to point up the "consumers surplus" problem we discussed earlier. One way of formalizing the concept of a "consumers surplus" that owners seek to protect is to raise the probability that owners will overvalue, and to lower, commensurately, the probability attached to undervaluing. Thus we could say that the probability of bidders' overvaluing remains one-half; but owners will overvalue two-thirds of the time and undervalue only in one-third of the cases. And, therefore, .833 of the properties will be overvalued (i.e., $1 - .5 [.33]$) . Owners will keep more than half the properties, and a higher proportion of their holdings will be overvalued. Hence a redistribution of tax liability from properties taken over by bidders to properties retained by initial owners will take place. This will happen whether there is a premium requirement on the take-over bid or not. But to the extent that there is such a requirement, the higher the premium is, the fewer will be the property transfers and the smaller the redistribution of tax liability.

The example just discussed deals, in essence, with "atomistic" valuing and bidding—the property is assessed by its owner and by one bidder. But this is only one of a number of possibilities and, indeed, not a highly realistic one. It lies at one extreme of the possible arrangements. At the other extreme is the situation in which both owners and bidders benefit from numerous assessments of their property. For bidders we might think of this as a real possibility if they formed syndicates or bidding groups, with each member of the large group estimating the value of each property and the group's decision rule being to bid the average of these estimates. For owners we could conceive of their forming voluntary associations to get numerous appraisals made of each of the properties of members of the association. Under the conditions each group should arrive at the same value for the property, with owners then declaring a value $V^*/(1 + X)$ as in earlier examples, except insofar as they wish to protect their "consumers surplus." This seemingly could be a substantial accomplishment compared to present achievements of property tax administration. But at what cost? Under the circumstances pictured here, the number of assessments and their cost would go up astronomically, say, by a factor of 200. (For calculating the expected value of $V^*/[1 + X]$ both assessing groups—the bidder's syndicate and the homeowner's association—would need, say, 100 appraisals of each property.)

Incidentally, owners might be able to protect their "consumers surplus" under self-assessment, and thus be able to value their properties at what they think their market value is, by arranging for "assessment insurance," under which, for a fee, they would be insured against a successful takeover bid on their property. This possibility, suggested to the authors by William Vickrey, serves to moderate the skepticism we expressed earlier about self-assessment because of the differential incorporation of "consumers surplus" in owners' valuations. The costs of such an insurance scheme would, of course, have to be reckoned in any comparison of S.A. with the more usual assessment schemes.

Other Problems

Inflation

Property values, like other prices, change, sometimes quite rapidly. This poses a problem for any assessment scheme. But for self-assessment it would be necessary, to prevent an inordinate amount of bidding and assessing, to develop simple procedures for adjustment of assessed values.

Under self-assessment, then, each year all property values could automatically be adjusted by some price index. Which one to use is debatable; none is perfectly suitable. But, as Strasma notes, any somewhat reasonable index is better than no adjustment, and the property owner has an automatic appeal in that he can declare a different value for his property if he so chooses.[17]

Uncertainty

Another possible objection is that self-assessment with forced sale would create greater uncertainty than government assessment and hence retard construction or improvements of land. Under government assessment there is a professionally assessed value (and tax liability based thereon) facing the developer (and developers can frequently get a prior indication of what that assessed value will be), whereas under self-assessment with forced sale (or penalty of some sort) there would be numerous potential assessors and hence a wide range of possible valuations. Even if the expected value of their bids was equal to the government assessor's valuation, the variance of this collection of bids would be greater and, therefore, so would the uncertainty surrounding the net returns from the investment. How serious a problem this represents is an empirical question.[18]

The Problem of Encumbrances

A seemingly severe obstacle to self-assessment is suggested by some of the legal writers in this field. This is the problem of separate rights and interests in real property which, according to Herrmann, "could pose potentially the greatest threat to the efficiency of any system of self-assessment."[19] It is a known fact that, for good economic reasons, the existence of encumbrances on land can seriously diminish the value of its potential use to any person contemplating bidding or taking title, as can the existence of leaseholds, reversionary interest, rights of entry, life estates, or the burden of restrictive covenants (as well as zoning). Land may also be pledged as security for debts.[20] Obviously, a bidder cannot abrogate these rights or interests merely by purchasing the basic or underlying estate. On the other hand, full recognition of all rights and interests may constitute such a set of constraints on the effective use of a property as to discourage bids, even though it be "underassessed." The problem, again in Herrmann's words, must be "resolved by balancing the expectation of parties prior to adoption of self-assessment and this past reliance on the inalienability of such rights and interests, with the probability of the future employment of grants of such rights or interests as a means of evading or totally avoiding the sanctions of the self-assessment system." (That the latter could be done is easy to envision. As mentioned above, imagine two fairly identical pieces of property owned by two different individuals. Each one could sell his respective property to the other for, say, $1.00 and lease it back for ninety-nine years for $1.00 a year. If the prospective bidder has to purchase either property subject to the lease, the property has little value to him, and the value for tax purposes is accordingly nil.)

To meet this problem, which is a difficult one—but one that must be solved if self-assessment is to work, especially in many larger municipalities—Herrmann proposes a two-step solution. The first step would be to require negotiation or recording of severable interests and rights in real property, as a condition precedent to recognition in the event of bid and purchase. This would notify the buyer of just what he is bidding on. The second and more radical step is to conceive of separate rights or interests in real property as being severable and as requiring separate declarations of value by persons who have duly recorded rights or interests in each given parcel of property. Property taxes would also be assessed on these declarations. Any bidder taking title of the underlying estate would take it subject to the rights or interests, but he would also be free to bid separately on them. The separate declarant would then have the option to sell or reassess with payment of a penalty.

The alleged benefits of such a solution are that it would have the salutary effect of merging interests and encouraging owner use and control of land, and that it would also result in the taxation of many interests and rights in real property which are, or could be, of more value than the basic or underlying estate itself. Our competence allows us to observe only that the problem of encumbrances must be dealt with if self-assessment is to be successful, but it is not clear that a property tax should get at those other interests as this solution proposes; and that there is a real problem here which serves to underscore the fact that any solution to the assessment problem, self-assessment included, will not be simple.

Conclusion

We have evaluated self-assessment and found a number of grounds for skepticism. One of the simplest but most basic is that the community may not permit the economic police work necessary for its effective operation. Measures varying from moral suasion and ostracism on up in severity may be taken against bidders. Taxpayer resentment is currently high and this in a situation where taxpayers are pitted against "government." If, in fact, they were to be pitted against their fellow citizens directly, the situation could be inflammatory. Or initial owner underassessment may be so great as to overwhelm the fiscal capacity that is available for bidding and taking over properties in the case of forced sale. The goals of self-assessment, we think, are more likely to be achieved under forced sale than if the owner is given an option to frustrate the bid, but incorporation of this latter feature will increase the likelihood of a community's accepting self-assessment.

But waiving this question of acceptance, we consider that a major deficiency of self-assessment lies not so much in the strong potential penalties that would be necessary to make it work, but the differential pattern of assessments (and also tax liability, of course) that would emerge as a result of property owners' efforts to protect against the penalties. In particular, owners who are less knowledgeable, more averse to risk, and less able to initiate and support search for alternative properties would be discriminated against. In reaching "consumers surplus" to a differential degree, self-assessment would result in different tax liabilities on properties of equal market value. And this is not a situation that taxpayers would consider fair. But neither do many of them consider the property tax as it is currently administered to be fair. So, more realistically, the relevant comparison is between self-assessment and a property tax employing government assessors. This latter tax currently is administered poorly, but can be improved. In our judgment, there is enough doubt about the efficiency of self-assessment and sufficient potential for improving current practice that one could argue that a major effort in this latter direction should take precedence over self-assessment as the next logical step in improving property tax administration. And we could add support for this judgment from the fact that self-assessment with forced sale constitutes a severe change in property rights, may be unconstitutional, and would run into deep problems with particular kinds of property, especially those that are encumbered.

However, one could argue the opposite, with some cogency. To make the case more positively for an experiment with self-assessment, we would say that we have become more inclined toward it as we have been impressed, by the other contributions to this volume, with how imperfect knowledgeable practitioners consider the current state of property tax administration. In the light of this desultory accomplishment after many years and the essentially nonprofessional personnel currently assessing in a large number of jurisdictions (more by number of jurisdictions and properties than by value of properties, but not insignificant even here), it could be argued that there is not so much to lose; self-assessment with forced sale may not be a strictly academic alternative.

We noted earlier that a self-assessment scheme with bids required to be at least 20 percent above the owner's valuation might not be supported by the community either because the sanction is too severe to be accepted by the public or because, if accepted, 20 percent is probably too low a cut-off to prevent sizable "hardship" for current owners—that is, some people who had valued honestly but low would not, with the proceeds from the forced sale of their properties, be able to purchase an equivalent one. However, suppose the premium was raised, so that, to be bona fide, a bid had to exceed the owner's valuation by at least 50 percent? In all likelihood, there would be much less opposition to self-assessment. A premium of this magnitude would seem considerably more reasonable and involve many fewer "hardship" cases. Fewer property owners would feel the need for outside appraisals, so the cost savings of self-assessment would be real. And property would be valued at 67 percent (and up) of its true value, which, by current standards, is quite an accomplishment. True, there will still be differential taxation of property depending on owners' knowledge, taste for risk or gambling, ability to undertake and support search, etc. But under the present system, too, the results are far from perfect. So all things being taken into account, self-assessment may deserve serious consideration.

On the more positive side, we simply note that a stronger case can be made for self-assessment as an interim device, while capacities and institutions for government assessment are being built up. This, in fact, is the context in which the revival of interest in self-assessment started. Self-assessment, whatever its imperfections, might be used by a developing country over a transitional period during which the administrative means would be developed for an adequate system of assessment by government fiscal officers. Administration of the tax could be lax, and the imperfections, like self-assessment itself, could be considered transitional. Yet it would be a great improvement over no tax on real estate or many current poor systems of government assessment. The important point here is that self-assessment would be easier to install initially, would establish the basis of some structure of valuation, and would mean that the government would begin to collect some revenue and begin to promote taxpayer awareness. These beginnings would ease the transition to subsequent, more sophisticated assessment schemes (if they can be implemented).

Finally, as Harberger has suggested, self-assessment could be a useful adjunct to current government assessment schemes as a relief device. He observed:

> Within a framework which stimulates high assessed values, the interests of the property owner can be protected by permitting him to make a bona fide offer of sale and to use as the assessed value in this case a figure of 20 percent below his offer price. Under this procedure a property owner is never required to be in the position of being *forced* to sell, although he may *voluntarily* place himself in that position if he considers the value put on his property by the assessing officers to be too high.[21]

In fact, we understand, some local jurisdictions in Florida have recently adopted a procedure along these lines. Taxpayers who object to an assessor's valuation of their property may state a value at which they think it should be assessed, and the jurisdiction has the right to offer it for auction at that price or a higher one.[22]

Acknowledgments

The authors wish to express their gratitude for helpful comments and suggestions from Henry Aaron, Charles Haar, Peter House, Wilbur Lewellen, William Letwin, Stewart Myers, Jeremy Shapiro, and William Vickrey. The authors also wish to thank the Sloan School of Management at the Massachusetts Institute of Technology for financial support toward the preparation of this paper.

Notes

1 Arnold C. Harberger, "Issues of Tax Reform for Latin America" in *Fiscal Policy for Economic Growth in Latin America,* Joint Program of the Organization of American States, Inter-American Development Bank, and Economic Commission for Latin America (Baltimore: Johns Hopkins Press, 1965), p. 120. This volume contains the papers and proceedings of a conference held in Santiago, Chile, December, 1962, and is hereafter referred to as *Fiscal Policy.*

2 John Strasma, who has developed a specific set of procedures for implementing self-assessment, notes that it could play a useful transitional role in jurisdictions that are engaged in longer-term programs to upgrade valuation staffs and to carry out cadastral surveys. See John Strasma, "Market-Enforced Self-Assessment for Real Estate Taxes—I," *Bulletin for International Fiscal Documentation,* September, 1965, p. 355.

3 Arnold C. Harberger, in *Fiscal Policy,* pp. 119–20. As an alternative to self-assessment with forced sale and as something that might accommodate "the objections of the lawyers," Harberger suggests (p. 119) that there be created "within the office in charge of property assessments, strong incentives against underassessment—penalizing assessment officers whenever properties assessed by them sell for prices substantially above the assessed value and rewarding assessment officers with 'good' records (i.e., whose assessed values turn out to be reasonably close to the actual sales prices of those properties which are sold)."

But this is not self-assessment and hence not within the scope of our paper. Moreover as John Strasma notes (*Bulletin for International Fiscal Documentation,* September, 1965, p. 362) apropos of this possibility, "But how to determine true transfer prices?"

4 *Fiscal Policy,* p. 422.

5 *Ibid.,* p. 133.

6 How big the reward for the frustrated bidder should be is an important question. Strasma, who would incorporate this option in his carefully spelled-out proposal for implementing a scheme of self-assessment, suggests a more severe penalty. To keep his property the owner would have to start to pay tax on the bid price and in addition pay a fine of double the annual tax difference; the frustrated bidder would get half of this sum, i.e.,

150 percent of the annual increment in tax liability resulting from his bid. See Strasma, *Bulletin for International Fiscal Documentation,* September, 1965, p. 403.

7 It has been suggested as an additional alternative to those enumerated that one way the government might make the threat credible would be to institute a system of checks and penalties similar to those used in the United States for the personal income tax; e.g., each person would submit his own assessed valuation and the government would spot-check some of these returns (the chance of an assessment's being audited increasing with the value of the property) and assess penalties if they were found to be inaccurate. This proposal, it seems to us, has one inherent defect, a defect not unique to self-assessment, but peculiarly severe to that system insofar as penalties are imposed for a divergence from "true" value. It assumes that in practice property values can be established as easily and objectively as monetary income can be measured. As will be pointed out in the text, this is not so.

8 The phrase "credible threat" is from Albert C. Hirschmann, "Land Taxes and Land Reform in Colombia," reprinted in Richard Bird and Oliver Oldman, *Readings on Taxation in Developing Countries* (Baltimore: Johns Hopkins Press, 1964), p. 422. He, in turn, got it from the "atomic strategists."

9 For a discussion of tax ferreting in Iowa, a system in which "ferrets" were rewarded by some fraction of the taxes due on property initially not reported by the taxpayer but uncovered by the ferret, see John E. Brindley, *History of Taxation in Iowa* (Iowa City: State Historical Society, 1911), I, 310–56. In Ch. 2 of this symposium, "Is the Property Tax Conceptually and Practically Administrable?" Harold Groves concludes that the experience with tax ferreting "seems to demonstrate that the ethics of tax administration cannot be maintained except by public officials under oath to follow the law."

10 Data in Table 12 of the *1960 Census of Housing, United States Summary,* I, 43, indicate that out of a total of 32,800,000 owner-occupied houses, 4,000,000 or 12.2 percent were moved into between January 1, 1959, and March, 1960, suggesting a rate of turnover of owner-occupied homes of about 10 percent per annum. The *1960 Census of Population, United States Summary,* I, 367 (Table 164), shows 47.3 percent of population five years of age or over (i.e., 75,000,000 people) not living in the same house as that they had lived in five years earlier. This figure, too,

suggests that a 10 percent turnover rate is of the correct order of magnitude.

11 Twenty percent of the market value of the property is $5000, which is just about equal to seventeen times $300.

12 "Inequality in Property Tax Assessment—New Cures for an Old Ill," *Harvard Law Review,* 75 (1962) , 1377n.

13 Oliver Oldman and Henry Aaron, "Assessment-Sales Ratio under the Boston Property Tax," *National Tax Journal,* March, 1965, p. 35.

14 Half of all two-family houses have assessment-sales ratios under one, and one-third of all two-family houses have ratios under one but greater than .8; i.e., one-third of all two-family homes have ratios that are no more than σ below the mean.

15 Since most proposals for self-assessment provide an alternative to forced sale, the consequence of random errors in valuation under this alternative would be differential ratios of assessed to true value for properties of the same true value.

16 John W. Pratt, "Risk Aversion in the Small and in the Large," *Econometrica,* 32 (January–April, 1964) , 123.

17 Strasma, *Bulletin for International Fiscal Documentation,* September, 1965, p. 355.

18 Of course, if the developer revalues his land to reflect the improvement, then self-assessment really presents no threat. This objection was originally raised in an agricultural context (Latin America) where it was feared a bidder could reap the profits from a good harvest as soon as it became obvious a good crop would be forthcoming. In an urban and industrial context, while still a problem, the threat may not be as serious.

19 Lawrence M. Herrmann, "A Possible Solution to the Valuation of Real Property in Latin America," unpublished, prepared for seminar on Land Reform in Developing Countries, Harvard Law School, June, 1964, p. 49.

20 These examples are mostly from Herrmann, *ibid.*

21 Harberger, in *Fiscal Policy,* p. 120.

22 This procedure, it should be remarked, may be a way of circumventing the legal problem connected with forced private sale and yet achieve substantially the same results. A governmentally sponsored public auction would enable the community to bring its full fiscal capacity—both public and private—to bear upon the underassessed property. The question remains, however, as to whether the community will support, or even allow, such an auction (see note 9 above) .

7 Anthony G. Ferraro

Valuation of Property Interests for *Ad Valorem* Taxation of Extractive Industry and Agricultural Realty: Problems and Solutions

In the valuation of both extractive interests and agricultural realty for *ad valorem* tax purposes, the fundamental concept of property taxation must be kept in mind. This concept, a legal and constitutional fact in most states, is that all property interests—real and personal—shall be taxable unless specifically exempt. Therefore, property rights of all types, including possessory rights and leasehold interests, will be discussed in this chapter.

The Appraisal of Extractive Industry

Definitions

Extractive land may be defined as that class of land which derives its value by the extraction or removal of products from it. It includes those categories of lands commonly known as mining claims, petroleum lands, coal mines, quarries, gravel and clay pits, mineral rights, and timber lands. Value is primarily a function of the market value of the products extracted, the cost of extraction, and the fact that the product extracted either is irreplaceable or requires a long period of time for replacement.

Most mineral lands are called "claims." A claim can be a quartz or a placer claim. An auxiliary piece of land, nonmineral in character, is known as a "millsite." It can be any land of five acres or less intended for milling installation or tailings deposits or for use as a mining campsite. A tunnel site claim is rarely used.

Claims may be patented or unpatented. If the claim is patented, actual title passes from the United States to the patentee. It is then subject to all the responsibilities of ownership claims, such as taxes. If the claim is unpatented, no title passes and only mining rights are transferred.

To acquire a mining right, first, one must make a discovery of a valuable mineral, and then, to retain this right, he must work and annually improve the claim. After $500 has been expended and one year's time has elapsed, a patent application may be filed.

A quartz claim covers vein or lode deposits. It may be developed by a shaft or tunnel. Such claims are normally 20.60 acres in extent, approximately 600 ft. by 1500 ft. If less than this, they are called "fractional claims." Only the mining rights of unpatented claims may be bought and sold; however, the claim must be worked each year to be retained.

Placer claims cover ground containing minerals in a loose state, which may be concentrated or collected by washing with water. These claims vary from 20 acres to 160 acres.

Land for milling, mining, storage rooms, boarding houses, cabins, bins, etc., is a millsite. If patented land, it is treated as industrial land. If it is unpatented, government regulations complicate appraisal. A millsite, like any industrial site, to have value must have adequate power at a reasonable rate, possess water, be accessible to rail or highway, and have utilities. The site should be level and higher than the tailing deposits to assure gravity flow and freedom from flood and snow slides. It should be centrally located and near a labor force and, preferably, free from smoke, dust, and fumes. Millsites may be held in conjunction with either quartz claims or placer claims.[1]

A mine may be defined as any unofficial excavation made to

extract mineral values. This would include both open-pit and underground workings, as well as quarries, oil, gas, and sulfur wells. Mines have value only when they contain a deposit from which a product can be extracted at a profit. The plant and equipment of a mine are of value only in proportion to its ability to produce ore. If ore cannot be mined profitably, the equipment is practically worthless. Minerals must be recovered to pay for the purchase price, the cost of development, including plant and equipment, all costs of operation and treatment —mining, milling, and marketing—and interest on the money invested, and to provide for both a profit for the operator, organizer, and investor and a payment as a lease royalty.[2]

Valuation of Extractive Industries

The methods of valuing extractive property have been greatly affected by technological changes, changing trends in supply and demand, taxation, legislation, production, price control, and the influence of labor organizations.

According to the United States Mineral Production statistics for 1964–66, the sand and gravel industry is the leading extractor, producing approximately 900,000,000 tons of sand and gravel annually. Second in mineral production is stone. Coal ranks third, followed by cement, iron ore, molybdenum, silver, salt, phosphate, and lime.[3]

The standard method of mineral valuation is to determine the present worth of estimated future earnings for the life of the property. From estimates of available ore, yearly output, and duration, the computed costs of extraction are deducted to determine an estimate of profit. Annual output multiplied by profit is used to arrive at annual income. The present worth of the future earnings is then calculated by application of an appropriate rate of return. This method of calculating the present value of future annuities from a wasting asset is commonly known as the "Hoskold Method" or "Hoskold Formula" and dates back to 1877.

The Hoskold Formula provides for the redemption of capital by use of an annuity fund, which is invested at a low, safe rate. When the mine is depleted, there will be a fund equal to the purchase price so that the operator can purchase another mine. "Hoskold" is generally accepted as a mining valuation tool and is still taught at most mining schools. Although present day usages and present day appraisers tend to disregard this method, it is one valid approach in determining the value of a wasting asset.

Psychological evaluation of consumer behavior is as important in successful mine operation as economic valuation. Perceptive analysis of the market for minerals is crucial since investment must be recaptured in a reasonable period of time. Next to faulty market analysis, inaccurate cost estimates are the greatest cause of mine failure. A subsidiary problem of the extractive industry is that of the tailings and residues of the mine.

Property adjacent to a producing mine also has current value. Otherwise reserves would have no value until extracted. Ore reserves normally are categorized as proven or inferred. Proven reserves are definite. Inferred reserves are ores that are believed to be there, or that can reasonably be expected to occur in the vicinity. These are normally discounted at least 50 percent. Reserves also need to be discounted for dilution and recovery percentage. The dilution allowance includes wall, rock, pillars, shafts, and an approximate 10 percent waste loss. The recovery percentage is used because ore recovery seldom reaches 100 percent of the ore in the mine. Mining costs are normally itemized as follows: development, direct mining, milling, transportation, and smelting.

The market—not the reserves—determines the amount of production. The faster the mineral is mined, the more profit is made. In the metalliferous industry, there are more risks and higher extractive costs than in a nonmetalliferous industry. A company's knowledge of proven reserves forms the basis for new equipment purchase decisions. If the reserves are nearing exhaustion, the company will repair and use old equipment.

Royalties.—Royalties are considered a form of distribution of profit between the operator and the fee owner. In the total valuation of the mine, the royalty portions of both the operator and the fee owner should be considered. Royalty may also be defined as the payment to the owner of a mineral right for the privilege of mining and producing the property. Royalty rates vary because of the time differences and conditions under which they were negotiated. They tend to be set low, so as not to retard or defer the development of the industry. Government royalties are set even lower than those on privately owned mineral lands. The prevailing rate of royalties on minerals, with adjustments, may be used as a standard of value of the minerals in the ground. This, however, does not reflect the operator's portion of the earnings: royalties are based only on the quantity, not the quality, of the product.

Interest rates.—Royalty is a prior lien on operating profits. The interest rate, on the other hand, is a return on a speculative investment; it is based on the operator's profits and therefore carries a higher risk rate than does royalty. Present thinking is that there should be an 8 percent to 10 percent interest rate, with hazards reflected in other factors, such as production and cost computations. While 8 percent to 10 percent is reasonable, sometimes 5 percent or 6 percent is used when the production and cost figures have been adjusted to cover the variables.

How various states treat the extractive industry.—The extensive experience of Michigan in mine valuation has shown that annual valuation of mineral property is desirable. Arizona's basis for assessing mines has been the Hoskold Formula, which measures the ultimate value of a mine as the profit over and above the cost of operation. However, because of concern about production variation through time and the inability of local assessors to value intangibles, Arizona is considering a formula based on yearly production. The State of Nevada uses net proceeds in lieu of *ad valorem* taxation.

The State of Idaho uses a production formula for valuing both producing and nonproducing mines. The State of West Virginia applies its business or occupational tax to extractive industries. Pennsylvania considers appraisal of mineral properties to be the responsibility of local tax assessors.

The State of Ohio treats the previous year's production from separately owned oil and gas rights as a criterion for determining the real property value of those rights, but coal and mineral deposits, like other property, are assessed at 40 percent of taxable value. The State of Utah is presently assessing valuable deposits on a reserve basis. However, this has not proven satisfactory since the method has too many intangibles, and a production formula is under consideration as an alternative.

The State of Colorado applies a production formula to determine tax on property used for metalliferous extraction, but nonmetalliferous property is valued in the same way as other property. The State of Montana taxes mines on a net proceeds basis. In Kentucky, production figures are submitted each year, and from these figures, assessments are recommended. If the valuation is not too easily defined, the assessment is based on the capitalization of royalty payments.

California assesses according to the capitalized earnings of the mine. This approach requires use of estimates of reserves, rate of mining income, net income, capitalization or discount rate, and special hazards. California, too, has established a mining committee to review and make recommendations as to future methods to be used in the valuation of extractive property.

Specific Comments

An analysis of sales of mining properties is very difficult because, first, there are very few sales of mines and, second, even when a mine is sold, comparisons are of limited value since no two mines are exactly alike. Most people feel that the only realistic approach to the valuation of extractive property is in terms of its income-producing potential. However, the mining industry generally feels that the use of a gross or net proceeds formula constitutes the levy of a severance tax. It is rather difficult to convince the industry that this is merely an appraisal method.

Extractive lands that are not assessed according to production are assessed at the discretion of the assessor, normally on the basis of an acreage figure. These acreage valuations are often established without regard for variation in the actual value of the land, the ability of the land to produce, and are not equalized with other valuations. In my opinion, there is no appraisal method more practical and equitable for determining a value for the assessment of a producing mine than one based upon proceeds. Valuation of mineral reserves is not an equitable tax base. The ultimate value of a mine is the value that can be realized from the extraction and marketing of a product, over and above the cost of doing so. It is usually impossible to evaluate an ore reserve satisfactorily. The mining owners rarely achieve an adequate valuation until the reserve is virtually exhausted. An underdeveloped mine has a speculative value until such time as exploration and development are undertaken. Its value may increase or decrease with development.

A second point to remember is that the assessment is on the mineral lands as real property—not on the ore extracted as such. While the value of the ore is used as a measure of value, it is the mine that is being valued. The tax levied by this valuation is not a severance tax, but is a tax upon the real property and is levied at the same rate as that for other real property. Mine machinery and surface improvements normally are valued separately. Underground improvements are included in the mine valuation.

Unpatented claims.—Many tax officials object to the assessments of unpatented claims, on the grounds that they are difficult to administer and that a tax lien on a possessory interest is almost impossible to enforce. Nevertheless, these claims are taxable under the law and should be valued.

Nonproducing patented mining claims.—Nonproducing patented mining claims are assessed at an acreage price. The valuation per acre is often frozen by tradition and bears no relationship to current value.

One of the difficulties with regard to the valuation of such mining claims is that they are often located in counties where the valuations were set many years ago, and there is a reluctance on the part of the assessor to reduce these values materially because they constitute a major part of the total valuation in the county. People do pay taxes on these high valuations

year after year. However, many of them are returned to the
county for delinquent taxes and some are resold, but many of
them never return to the roll because of these high and obso-
lete valuations.

Severed mineral reserves.—Distinct from mining claims are
rights to such minerals as oil and gas. The ownership of these
rights is separated or severed from the ownership of the surface. Mineral rights may have been reserved by the federal government or by state and county governments. Privately owned
mineral rights also are severed from surface ownership. They
are subject to taxation as separate property, even though there
may be no evidence of the presence of minerals.

Classification of mines.—The problem of classifying the
product of any given mine for a valuation on the basis of production is a fundamental one. Most statutes do not make clear
which products are metalliferous or precious metals and which
are other types.

A more equitable distribution between the mine that has
production and the number of acres to be included should also
be made. In some cases, when a nonproducing claim is con-
verted to a producing claim, it is possible for the assessment to
be lowered because of the division over a greater number of
acres. There should perhaps be a provision that no assessment
of a mine that is a producing mine may be less than the assessment on the claims included before the mine was classified as
producing.

Conclusion

The full cash value of extractive land is difficult to determine. It depends upon the future market value of the product
when and if extracted, and this value can be known only after
a product has been extracted. The market value of extractive
property is not a useful assessment guide. Sales of such land
are infrequent. Furthermore, even though the market value of
one unit of extractive land may be known, it is impossible to
determine accurately the probable market value of others by
comparison. Therefore, the only feasible method of determining the value of such property is on the basis of actual produc-

tion. Since property of this category is subject to depletion, production value should be assessed only once as it occurs. No more equitable basis of assessment can be suggested at this time than that of capitalization of net proceeds.

The owner of each producing unit of extractive land should be required to file with the assessor an annual statement of production. Possessory rights, leasehold interests in public lands, and severed mineral rights should all be subject to assessment. If lands that are classified for purposes of assessment as extractive lands, whether producing or not, have in addition a use which is either agricultural or situs in nature, the value of that additional use should be taken into consideration in assessing the land. All the intangibles used in the Hoskold Formula, such as value of ores, value of reserves, time to remove ore, capitalization rate, hazards, etc., are automatically recognized and considered in the annual production formula.

The Banner Mining Company recently closed its underground copper mines in New Mexico because of increased mining costs. The mine had been operated profitably since 1935 but began losing money during the last two years of operation. Clearly mining companies do not and cannot operate at a loss. Therefore, when they are operating profitably is the proper time for their market value to be appraised according to percentages of their gross or net income.

Ideally, all extractive lands should be under a state severance tax. Lacking this uniform approach, states should appraise according to capitalization of the net profit as the next best approach. However, since most states must develop a solution within limits of consitutional hodgepodge, gross or net production figures realistically applied will suffice.

The Appraisal of Agricultural Realty

In appraising agricultural realty, only the comparative or sales approach and the income approach are applicable. The pure and uncomplex agricultural unit of years ago is gone forever. Today there exists an interplay of economic forces that complicates the valuation process. "Highest and best use" may be other than the present use. This may not be an appealing argument to present owners, but it is an economic fact. Owner-operated farms and ranches today are marginal, because the economic units have changed. A ranch now, to make profitable use of land and machinery, must be at least a 300-cow unit, with various combinations of leased public lands and private or fee ownership. The small ranch or farm, like the individual grocer, is becoming a "thing of the past."

Land devoted to agricultural interests must be distinguished from agricultural land being turned toward urban, commercial, or recreational development. For tax purposes on agricultural realty, one must value the physical wealth and exclude financing and equity interests that are tied to management. Income and sales must be confined to the agricultural components. All other influences or uses should be differentiated and separately valued.

Let us examine the national evolution that has created the present problems in agricultural realty appraisal. Because of the ample documentation and fairly representative situations, we will take Colorado as an example for most comparisons.

The Agricultural Land Market

Land prices.—Rural land prices in Colorado increased 6 percent last year, while the average in other states was 8 percent. Colorado's irrigated land increased 3 percent, and dry farming land was up 8 percent. This equaled gains in Wyoming and Utah, but was less than the 11 percent gain in Arizona. Grazing land values in Colorado increased 8 percent, exceeded only by those in New Mexico with an 11 percent increase.[4]

Land demand.—The price of cattle ranches in the West is difficult to analyze. There are few bargains for ranchers in the United States. Very few cattle ranches sell for their cash economic worth. There is a demand for large ranches from high-salaried business executives and from companies seeking to diversify. Prices have reached the point where a cattleman, depending solely on the income from the operation, has difficulty competing for available land. Continual increases in land prices have occurred, despite the largest spread in history between wholesale and retail beef prices. Land prices have advanced 60 percent more than income between 1954 and 1964.

Interest rates.—Market forces have steadily reduced the rate at which land earnings are capitalized. There is evidence from appraisal reports and from market data that the effective market capitalization rate has declined over the last ten years. Price acceleration has reduced the rate of return. A federal survey of eighty-five representative ranches indicates that the average rate of return is 2 percent.[5]

Reasons for Price Trend

Population.—People make land valuable, and population increase is one of the most important factors affecting the market price of range land. Projections through 1975 indicate that the population increase in the eleven western states will be double that of the national average. Annually, 2,000,000 acres of land in the United States are required for the development of cities, highways, reservoirs, etc.; 67 percent of this is Class I and Class II agricultural land. The same population growth that has helped the beef cattle industry to grow is now pushing the beef ranches out of the prime valley lands into the hills and brush country.

Nonranch uses.—Land acquisition by the federal government or by state and community projects is seriously curtailing the available supply of western land. Land is fixed in supply, and more land is being appropriated for public purposes each year. Eventually the remaining private land will be unable to support the tax burden.

Hedge against inflation.—Because the supply of land is fixed, it has been a traditional hedge against inflation. Periods of high economic activity and inflation are conducive to investments in agricultural lands. However, the available supply of land is decreasing, while the demand for it is increasing since many investors feel it is more stable than some of the other traditional types of investments.

Additions to present holdings.—One of the principal purchasers of agricultural realty is still the man next door. His original holdings were purchased at low prices or inherited, and he can justify the high price paid by averaging his entire spread. Since economic units are becoming larger, he feels that he can handle larger properties with the same amount of equipment.

Tax advantage.—Owners of agricultural lands that are being sold at subdivision prices may trade for other agricultural lands to avoid paying capital gains taxes at that particular time. Such exchanges are driving the price of range land upward. The lower tax rate applicable to capital gains, as opposed to ordinary income, contributes to the premium that buyers in the high tax bracket are willing to pay for future capital appreciation. Current income from the property has little or nothing to do with the purchase price. In many areas the advantage, from the standpoint of real property taxes and personal taxes, is substantial in that agricultural lands are still consistently and traditionally given lower assessed valuations than other types of realty.

Terms of payment and financing.—Prepaid interest transactions appear to be driving the market level higher than it would be under the more typical financing arrangements.

Depreciation.—Nonagricultural purchasers may allocate the sales price. Attempts are made to lose money in "depreciation" to remain in a favorable tax bracket. And since the sale often includes land, improvements, cattle, and equipment, the non-farm items are often overvalued at the expense of the real property.

Social desirability.—People want to own land even if, in many cases, they cannot make profitable use of it. Real estate has been everyone's favorite investment since the beginning of time. It has the positive appeal of tangibility.

Irrigation development.—Lands formerly used for grazing are now developed to irrigation. One of the important effects of this has been that forage crop production has shifted from some of the best to some of the worst lands, thus releasing the good soils for more valuable, deep-rooted crops.

Demands for particular types of ranches.—In Utah high prices are paid for spring range because of its scarcity. In Nevada sagebrush grazing land is purchased by those who desire to trade it to the federal government for lands that are better suited to their operation. Speculators and land promoters are buying large areas of agricultural land and selling it off in small blocks at nominal prices per acre. People, especially easterners, are buying plots of western land that they have never seen. Justifiable or not, these promotions are affecting the market value of all lands in those areas.

Recreational and residential uses.—Both recreational and residential uses of land have increased at a greater rate than any other land use. The average citizen, with more free time to spend on recreational activities, has stimulated the conversion of wildlife and grazing areas into recreational facilities. Such developments have reduced the land area available, and property values have risen accordingly. It is estimated that recreational use of such lands will increase forty times between 1956 and the year 2000.

Accessibility.—Lands in the West are becoming more accessible. More and better roads, faster automobiles, and speedier public transportation have permitted an influx of people; and it is people that give land its value.

Government subsidies.—Most agricultural lands qualify for government subsidies. An owner can receive up to 50 percent of the cost of many of his farm or ranch improvements. These payments tend to increase prices.

A way of life.—Despite the economic evolution, many people raised in the agricultural business desire to continue, regardless of the monetary return. Many think that the ranch or the farm is the only place to raise children.

Outside income.—Many farmers and ranchers are able to lease out hunting and fishing privileges, in addition to oil rights, which provide an important source of revenue.

Supply and demand—All the foregoing reasons for the increase in agricultural prices point to what is probably the most important of all—the old law of supply and demand. On the one side, we have the strong demand for land to enlarge ranches as an inflationary hedge, and, on the supply side, we see offerings restricted by taxes on capital gain. The highest price seems to be paid by segments of the market other than those interested in farming or ranching. Therefore, it seems that the "highest and best use" of this land may be not for agriculture but as a commodity or a medium of exchange, and much of its value may come from the extent that it can increase the value of other lands or a whole enterprise. As inflation causes the purchasing power of the dollar to decrease annually, land becomes safer than dollars, and, under these circumstances, it is reasonable to expect that agricultural land prices will continue to increase.

Assessment Problem Areas

The income approach.—The income approach requires that accurate data with respect to income and expenses be gathered and analyzed. However, ranchers and farmers seldom keep good records over a period of years. They are notorious for living off the land, often listing expenses for food, vehicles, and even entertainment. Advanced technology has outdated past earnings and cost trends as assessment criteria. Rental information of neighborhoods, especially cash rental rates, should be established. Then valuable crops and forage rentals must be determined. The landlord-approach method of developing value is a more realistic one involving less risk than that of attempting to evaluate influence of management by using owner-operator statements.

The ratio of crops shared between landlord and tenant is an old-fashioned idea. Today, huge investments in equipment, especially Valley Sprinklers approximating $25,000 to $30,000, must be recognized. With such expenditures, labor is reduced and operating expenses are increased. Therefore, crop ratios must be realigned. The traditional way is not the proper way. The proper way would be to compute income and expenses and apportion them between the respective parties.

When the income approach is used in the valuation of agricultural lands, two major factors requiring consideration are the salary of the manager and the proper rate to be used in capitalization of net income. Other factors should also be considered, such as tax advantages and pride of ownership. In some cases, the purchaser of an agricultural unit will consider that, when he buys the unit, he is buying himself a job as well. This major consideration cannot be compared to investment in stocks or bonds or in a parcel of real estate.

Other factors which permit an indirect income to the agricultural operator, in the form of moneys or amenities, are depreciation allowances, a hedge against inflation, the advantages given by the government conservation program, and income he may receive from leased lands involved in the operation of the ranch.

The market data approach.—When the comparability of sales is being considered, differences in such variables as price per acre, location, amount of water, improvements, climate, and soils should be analyzed. People with money and desire make value. The appraiser doesn't make value; he finds it in the market. For example, in Colorado the market indicates that a cow unit will cost between $800 and $1200.[6]

Agricultural landowners have traditionally stated that it is always the outsider coming into the state or area who drives the price of land upward. Contradicting this statement are the growth of grazing associations and the tremendous land purchases made by them. Grazing associations and cooperatives are limited to the Great Plains area. They are nonprofit corporations formed by local people interested in land reform. The preponderance of the members of these associations are farmers, and their slogan is, "Use products instead of selling them." Only farmers engaged in crop-farming may become members. The FHA will loan members 100 percent of the market value of their property. The interest rate approximates 4¾ percent, and the loan is serviced by the FHA. The FHA loans to the association up to a maximum of $2,000,000 and then may loan as much as $60,000 to the individual. The FHA in appraising the properties uses market value based on sales, but the association itself, comprising the local farmers and ranchers, buys the land according to productivity. The loan is amortized over a forty-year period. As of 1966, there were approximately twenty such associations in Colorado including some 650 agricultural families.

Capitalization rate.—It is my personal feeling, although there are other methods of determining the capitalization rate, that the rate must be determined from the market. Regardless of subjective opinions, only from the market do we obtain an objective rate which reflects the thinking of people who are developing this market. There is absolutely no relationship between a capitalization rate and interest money for other necessities, such as livestock and machinery. The capitalization rate is the return that a typical buyer expects. Landowners traditionally contend that land has no value; however, land is always worth at least its rental value, and, furthermore, all land has capitalized value. If an operator cannot make a profit, he should recognize that he is the marginal operator and should let someone else do it. The market today is set, regardless of the motives and regardless of increases for the future. Most investors in agricultural lands are satisfied with a low 2 percent return, because they expect land values to go up an average of 5 percent a year, giving them a total return of approximately 7 percent.

Farm improvements.—The need for and use of agricultural improvements should be considered in land appraisal. Their contribution to the overall operation and the question of what is typical for the operation should be evaluated. An exception to this is the appraisal of residential units. Residential units are needed for shelter and have an amenity value to the occupants. This need is universal, and, therefore, I am opposed to discounts for residential improvements on farmsteads. The other problem in improvements appraisal is the typical reluctance of the assessor to consider obsolescence when farm improvements no longer supply their need or no longer are necessary.

Leasehold interests.—Public-land leases to individuals are valuable and desirable from an economic standpoint. Evidence of their value is that most loan companies are willing to make substantial loans with these permits as collateral. In general, public leases bring approximately one-fifth to one-tenth the rent charged on civilian leases for identical types of land. These leases have evidence of value when sold in the market.

They may be purchased outright or the value may be capitalized into deeded land to which the grazing permits are attached.

Grazing fees on the United States forest lands are established from a base year of 1931, depending on the parity and selling price of livestock from the preceding year. In Colorado, the fees are approximately sixty cents per month for cattle and fifteen cents for sheep.

The Bureau of Land Management permits are fees established by the average price of beef and lamb on the western markets for the preceding year. These fees approximate thirty-three cents for cattle and six and a half cents for sheep. Most of these permits go with the land when the land is sold. In addition to these two types of land, there are also state school lands and Indian lands.

In Colorado, the average rental paid for school grazing land is approximately thirty cents an acre. The only way that a rancher can acquire a permit for these grazing rights is either to buy the permit or to buy the land.

In the appraisal of ranches, the matter of leased land is of primary importance. On many ranches, leased land may be the the major portion of the total ranch, while the deeded land may represent a relatively small percentage. A landowner who controls leased public lands has a leasehold interest on this land; he has a favorable advantage between the contract rent that he pays and the economic rent, and he derives a benefit or an annual income from this leased land. The value of the contract rental is the present worth of the capitalized difference between economic rent and contract rent.

Recently in Wyoming a study of right-of-way property, conducted by the Federal Highway Division, indicated that 25 percent to 40 percent—approximately eight to ten dollars per acre—was added to the sales price of the fee land to cover the effect of the leasehold interests. Near Delta, Colorado, Taylor Grazing Rights or Bureau of Land Management lands sold amounted to thirty-six dollars per animal-unit month.

Recently the Virginia Supreme Court rendered a decision affirming that leasehold interests were subject to tax and stating that, whenever an interest in land, whether freehold or for a period of years, is severed from the public domain and is put into private lands, the natural implications are that it goes there with the ordinary incidents of private property and therefore is subject to tax. Leasehold interests have value and should be assessed. It is sad to say that this property right has been ignored in Colorado and, I would dare say, in most of the other states.

Water rights.—Water is the lifeblood of western agricultural land. Yields will increase if water is available to apply at the critical time. Water rights are classified according to duration of supply, those for a full season or those granting ample water for an appropriate, specified period of time being most valuable. Cities needing domestic water have paid up to $350 per acre-foot of water. Colorado State University researchers studying water-value relationships in northeastern Colorado concluded that an acre of land increased twenty-one dollars in value for every acre-foot of water added. Water represents 80 percent of the farmland value.

Impact of recreation.—Recreation is big business and is getting bigger every year. As the length of the average working week decreases, more and more dollars will be spent on leisure pastimes. The increase in population and automation, more rapid and convenient travel, and higher income also encourage more recreation. Population increases in particular will have a great impact on recreation: the increase in the western states will be approximately 148 percent in the next decade. Colorado's population is expected to increase 59 percent and California's 75 percent between now and 1970, according to predictions made in 1965.

It is a natural step from an appraisal of rural properties to the appraisal of recreational lands. The economic fact is that there is less and less farm and ranch land left in the West that can be valued on the basis of cash returns and productivity. There is a growing scarcity of recreational land also. The amount of land usable for recreation is fixed, and each year some of the best land is taken for urban development.

There have been startling increases in prices following

public acquisition or proposed public acquisition. Speculators, often knowing in advance that certain lands will be condemned, buy up the land in these new areas. In the Delaware Water Gap National Recreational Area, three hours' time from the New York–Philadelphia area, land selling for $100 an acre five years ago is now on the market at $5000 an acre. At the Flaming Gorge National Recreational Area of Utah, the Bureau of Reclamation originally appraised land at thirty-nine dollars an acre. Shortly after the government began to purchase the land, the prices rose, eventually reaching $929 per acre.[7]

From an appraiser's standpoint, recreational lands must be recognized as such. One test is to attempt to identify that portion of the property value which appears to be in excess of the cash economic value. Not all income is cash. Part of the income is the intangible gains derived from certain amenities, and these gains include the increment of value created by the land's potential for recreational uses.

A dramatic example of the effect of recreation on land values has been the development of ski areas in Colorado and neighboring western states. Most of the ski lands belong to the Forest Service. However, in order to develop a ski area, land for ski operations, parking, and utilities is necessary. Additional land is also needed for service areas. Almost all ski area developments are based on low-priced bare land acquisitions or on leased or public lands, but adjacent to these ski areas privately owned fee land can be developed as resort areas. In the western states, agricultural grazing meadows are often valued at thirty to fifty dollars an acre. However, between the period of 1958 and 1965 ski area developers acquired such grounds at prices ranging from $200 to $1300 an acre.

One of the most impressive illustrations of this intensive growth has been the creation of the completely new city of Vail, Colorado. Five years ago Vail Village was a sheep pasture. Today it is an internationally known ski resort with $27,500,000 invested. Recently news was released that a new subdivision or suburb called "Big Horn" will be developed. Five hundred acres have been subdivided into 250 building sites, each costing from $4000 to $6000, and the area is already more than 75 percent sold out.

Urban influences.—The most difficult appraisal assignment is to determine the value of so-called urban influences on fringe land, or "rurban land." The methods used to determine this value must depend on the legislation, constitutional intent, and the politics of the pressure groups in individual states.

From an appraisal standpoint, if the intent is to develop market value, then the "highest and best use" principle must govern. This means that the value of the agricultural lands should be applied and then the urban influences extracted and measured, depending upon the time element for developing the property. The present worth of this value can be discounted and measured.

Summary and Conclusions

In the valuation of agricultural realty, external influences should be recognized and separately valued, especially rurban, residential, and recreational. The landlord method of developing value should be used rather than the owner-operator method. A capitalization rate should be taken from the market if it is to be realistic. A useful rate cannot be concocted by the "band of investment" or other academic methods. Farm improvements should be valued according to their contribution to total value. Rural residential units provide the same shelter requirements as urban units. Public land leases have value and should be assessed and taxed *ad valorem*. Water rights and availability must be measured.

Owners of agricultural land are vocally strong and well organized. When sales time occurs, they want all of the modern, economic factors to apply. However, from a tax standpoint, they are exponents of status quo and desire to keep things as they were in the "good old days."

In conclusion, it should be recognized that the problems of property taxation of both the extractive industry and agricultural realty are not insurmountable and are administratively solvable. The solutions depend upon the political climate, the integrity and intent of the administrator, and whether or not he has the capacity to face up to his administrative responsibilities.

Notes

1 Ernest Oberbillig, "Appraisal of Mineral Lands," *The Appraisal Journal*, October, 1964, pp. 485–521.

2 T. J. Hoover, *Economics of Mining* (Stanford: Stanford University Press, 1933), p. 21.

3 United States Bureau of Mines, "United States Mineral Production Statistics 1964–1966," *Mining Engineering*, February, 1967, p. 72 (reprinted from data of U.S. Bureau of Mines, *Commodity Data Summaries*, January, 1967).

4 United States Department of Agriculture, *Farm Real Estate Market Developments*, (Washington, D.C.: Economic Research Services, July, 1966), pp. 3–43.

5 Walter F. Willmette and Robert W. Ford, "Range Land and Cattle Ranch Appraisal, Course V," presented at American Institute of Real Estate Appraisers, June 3–10, 1967, Granby, Colorado.

6 Jack Guinn, "Gamble on Grass: The Story of Cattle in Colorado," *Denver Post*, January 8, 1967, Empire Sec., p. 9.

7 United States Department of the Interior, *Recreational Land Price Escalation*, (Washington, D.C., 1967), p. 10.

Frederick D. Stocker

Assessment of Land in
Urban-Rural Fringe Areas

There has been for a number of years a growing concern over the question of how undeveloped land in urban-fringe areas should be assessed and taxed. The question has puzzled policy makers and property tax administrators alike. The legislatures of many states have produced what they regard as an answer to this problem. In a few states the people have expressed themselves via referenda. Likewise, over the years I have occasionally expressed my own analysis and opinions on the topic. In line with the theme of this symposium, I will here concentrate on the administrative aspects of the property tax as it applies to urban-fringe property.

For as long as there has been a property tax (at least, one levied *ad valorem*), there have been problems over the valuation of property for which a new and more profitable use is emerging. When relatively few properites or property owners were involved, the problem could be and largely was ignored. This is no longer the case. The forces and processes that we describe by the word "urbanization" have, as one of their effects, made nearly every acre of land for miles around every sizable city a potential site for construction of homes, an industrial plant, or a shopping center.

This phenomenon underlies the dramatic rise in farm land values. It has added to our national wealth, at least in the sense that the dollar value of the nation's land has greatly increased. It has added little, I would say, to the assessed values placed on undeveloped land in most affected areas; the prevailing practice has been for assessors to minimize those elements in value that reflect speculative considerations or prospective changes in use. Urban expansion has added greatly, however, to the headaches of the assessor and of those responsible for tax policy making.

The headaches in assessing and taxing land in urban fringe areas have at least three causes. First of all, such properties represent a classic case of the divergence of market value from current earning capacity of the land. Instances in which property values have become excessive in relation to current return have always given rise to the charge that the property tax is unfair and have led to the search for relief, as in the form of homestead exemptions, exemption of certain kinds of intangibles, and inventory tax exemption. Such remedies, I would suggest, imply a fundamental distrust of property value as a basis for fair apportionment of a sizable part of the tax load. However that may be, the fact remains that strict application of the *ad valorem* principle to the assessment of urban-fringe property has frequently been condemned as unfair.

A second element of the problem is the general belief that a strict *ad valorem* assessment policy would have undesirable land use consequences. This belief rests on the supposition that many owners of undeveloped land may be forced by rising taxes to sell off lots piecemeal, thereby ruining the area for subsequent planned development and incidentally reducing their own opportunity to obtain the maximum profit from sale of their land.

A third difficulty in assessing and taxing urban-fringe land is the administrative problem. It is extremely difficult, for reasons I shall examine later, to place an accurate appraisal on land that lies in a transition zone—land that is economically something more than farm land but still something less than a building site. Still harder it is to keep assessments current on the dynamic, growing edge of a metropolitan area. In many an urbanizing county the job of adequately keeping on top of values in the urban fringe could well absorb the entire staff at the assessor's disposal.

Establishing a rational and effective policy for valuing fringe-area property has been complicated by two deep-seated and powerful attitudes. One is the esteem and sympathy a large part of the general public feels toward the farmer. We live, after all, in a society of which a large portion is only one or two generations away from the farm—far enough, in other words, to blur the distasteful aspects of farm life, but close enough to keep alive nostalgic and often idealized remembrances of the bucolic life. I think it quite possible that the careworn and harassed urban apartment dweller is a more earnest advocate of the preservation of farming as a way of life than is the dirt farmer himself.

Let me add here parenthetically that not all the land in urban-fringe areas, by a long way, is or ever was owned by the man who plows and harvests it. Much, of course, is not farm land at all in any realistic sense. And much of what is farm land is owned by absentee owners—perhaps descendants of a previous owner-operator, but often local or absentee investors. The owner-operator, whom we are inclined to think of as "typical," may be very much in the minority.

The other attitude with which policy makers have had to reckon is the growing public concern over preservation of open spaces. This concern has been most pronounced, and its spokesmen most influential, in the most urbanized states—that is to say, in the states where one would expect the voice of agriculture to be weak. Alarm is expressed not over the phenomenon of urban growth as such, but over the pattern of growth—haphazard and unplanned, as connoted by the term "urban sprawl." Many residents of urbanized areas have seen in this trend the imminent vanishing of the countryside as they once knew it.

It is, of course, a time-honored American custom, whenever a social or economic problem is perceived, to seek the solution in some kind of tax gimmick. Thus the idea quickly developed that urban sprawl could be averted, and open spaces preserved in their pristine state, by simply holding down assessed values, on the old theory that, if high taxes on undeveloped land speed the land into higher (more productive) uses, lower taxes would retard this movement.

In many states, majorities in the legislature and in the electorate have apparently been persuaded that tax abatement would safeguard open spaces from urban encroachment. The result has been the enactment in perhaps one-third of the states of some form of tax preference for urban-fringe land. I shall not attempt here to consider in detail the various approaches; this has been done in reports of the U.S. Department of Agriculture and the Council of State Governments.[1] To speak of these laws in broad generalities, I would note four characteristics: (1) Most have been limited to land "used in agriculture." (2) Most have taken the form of a requirement that assessors, in valuing such land, take account only of factors relevant to agricultural use. (3) Only a few have provided for recapture of any part of the back taxes, in the event the land is developed. (4) Only a few have coupled tax abatement with any binding restriction on future use of the land.

How are we to evaluate the policy of giving preferential tax treatment to land or farm land in the urban fringe? Any evaluation is necessarily a personal judgment representing a subjective balancing of antithetical considerations that relate to tax equity, economic effects, and administration. I will give my own evaluation.

First, I cannot agree with the view that rejects preferential measures out of hand as violations of either or both of two fundamental principles of the property tax—the *ad valorem* principle and the *ad rem* principle. A judgment cannot properly be rendered, in my view, simply by invoking an abstract principle; it is essential to look to the practical consequences of the policies in question.

On grounds of tax equity, I regard preferential tax treatment as a legitimate effort to smooth one of the rough edges of the property tax, to align the tax burden more closely with the owner's "ability to pay" as reflected in the current income from the property. Where tax preferences are often objectionable is in their failure to limit their benefits to the specific groups intended. Proponents typically stress the plight of the farmer who is struggling to meet his growing tax load out of a modest and often not growing farm income. But it is difficult to ease his tax load without simultaneously subsidizing the land speculator or developer.

Charges of inequity may also be made with respect to the singling out of one group for tax relief while others less numerous or less influential continue to pay property taxes that may be far out of proportion with their ability to pay.

As to the economic effects of preferential tax treatment, the principal questions concern influences on land use. To expect tax abatement alone, without other direct land-use controls, to lead a more desirable pattern of land use (i.e., preservation of open spaces) strikes me as excessively optimistic. The inducement of an opportunity for quick profit on sale of land is far too powerful to be countered by the mere prospect of protection from rising taxes.

The administrative aspects of the property tax as applied to urban-rural fringe land are especially significant; in view of the emphasis of this symposium, I want to consider administration in some detail. What are the administrative problems of land valuation in urban-fringe areas? And to what extent do preferential assessment laws resolve or bypass these problems?

There are serious administrative problems in establishing an *ad valorem* assessment for undeveloped land in transition areas. For farm properties in the rural-urban fringe, such criteria of assessment as a capitalization of potential farm earnings or farm rental value give no true indication of market value. The source of value for properties of this kind lies not in their current use or production, but in the competition of buyers who see in undeveloped land a prospect either for capital gain in a later resale or for profit through developing the land themselves. The only indication the assessor has of the market value of land in a market dominated by such motives consists of information on prices at which comparable properties have actually sold.

There are, however, both conceptual and practical difficulties in attempting to judge the market value of land in the rural-urban fringe by the sale prices of the few properties that are sold. These difficulties are quite apart from the usual problems of obtaining information for a large enough number of sales and of screening out transactions that do not reflect an "arms-length" bargain.

The comparable sales method of assessment is based on the economic principle that in a homogeneous market there is, at any given time, one and only one price. Even though there may be only a few transactions in the market during that period, the price at which they occur establishes the going market price and hence the price at which any other single item in the market (though not all) could have sold. This price thus becomes the market value of any other essentially similar item in the market.

But consider the nature of the market that works so neatly to establish a single, universally pertinent value. The principle just described applies only in what the economist calls a "perfect" market, and the perfect market must meet certain conditions: (1) It requires a homogeneous product—every item in the market indistinguishable (at least in any relevant economic respect) from any other. (2) The number of individual items in the market should be, for practical purposes, limitless. (3) The number of individual buyers and sellers is assumed to be so large that no one of them alone has the power to affect the market price. No single buyer or seller, in other words, dominates the market. (4) All buyers and sellers are assumed to have full and equal access to the market, including especially full knowledge of the market.

Other conditions could be mentioned, but these are the significant ones. Let us examine each in turn, from the viewpoint of its applicability to the market for farm land in rural-urban fringe areas.

First, do we have a homogeneous commodity in the land market in the rural-urban fringe? Obviously not. Each undeveloped tract around a growing city, though it may be similar to others in fertility and other agricultural characteristics, has unique locational attributes. Location is indeed likely to be the most significant single value-determining factor. Also, the individual parcels of property vary in size. The advantage to the large-scale developer of being able to obtain a single tract large enough to suit his needs means that a large tract under a single ownership may be worth more in an urban-oriented market than would the same acreage in the hands of a number of separate owners. Similarly, the price an owner can obtain for his property often depends upon whether his neighbor is also willing to sell. Unique considerations of this sort impair the validity of market price data as an indicator of the value of other properties.

If the market is not homogeneous, neither is it limitless. Both demand and supply of undeveloped land have definite limits in any area at any particular time. Demand is limited by the rate at which urban expansion is occurring. Except in the most rapidly growing metropolitan areas, conversion of one large tract to residential use, instead of proving that nearby land can now be sold at a comparable price for similar use, may exhaust the demand for residential sites for some years. Likewise the supply is not unlimited. Ordinarily there are only a few choice locations for residential, commercial, or industrial development. When these tracts are taken up, the nature of the market for remaining properties differs sufficiently that records of the sale prices on the tracts that were sold may have little relevance to the value of those that remain.

Nor, in the typical rural-urban fringe market, is the number of separate buyers and sellers large enough to approximate the economist's "perfect market." Usually only a few developers or investors actively buy up land. Also there may be only a few owners of farm land in the areas where development is taking place.

More important, knowledge of market conditions may be very limited. Buyers may be unaware of properties that could be bought, and sellers may be unaware of the possibilities for selling. In either case, the effect is to introduce imperfections that tend to undermine the validity of sale price as an indicator of market value.

Furthermore, the use of sale prices as a guide to market value assumes that the market is static. Only in a market where values are not changing does it make sense to regard a sale price at one time as indicative of value at some later time. But the land market in the rural-urban fringe is usually highly dynamic. Indeed, as I have noted, one sale may radically change the entire market situation. In a constantly changing market, a sale at one point in time may reveal little or nothing about value at another—even of the same property, to say nothing of those considered to be more or less comparable.

In many segments of the real estate market, data on comparable sales are no doubt the most reliable indicator of market value available to the assessor. Of course, they must always be used with care and discretion. In the rural-urban fringe, however, the land market is both so imperfect and so dynamic that sale prices must be interpreted with extreme caution in establishing assessed values.

In view of the difficulties involved in obtaining an *ad valorem* assessment of urban-fringe land, it might be expected that legislation establishing a different assessment standard for these properties would simplify matters. In a way it does; the practical consequence of laws calling for assessment of farm land at "agricultural-use" values usually is simply the continuation of the status quo. Legislation serves to legalize what many assessors do anyway—that is, to hold assessments on undeveloped land unchanged until a change in use actually occurs.

But such a policy hardly qualifies as good tax administration. Use-value assessment laws presumably require an effort from the assessor to determine the value that land would have if all nonagricultural factors are ignored. How is the assessor to do this? Sale prices of nearby tracts are explicitly ruled out. Sale prices of farm land located beyond the range of urban influence, if any can be found, are not truly comparable, because agricultural value itself is likely to be influenced by proximity to an urban center. Capitalization of earnings presents all the familiar problems, including especially that of selecting an appropriate capitalization rate. Rates of return on agricultural land, even in areas far from urban influences, are notoriously low in relation to those on other assets.

A more serious administrative problem concerns the responsibility that is placed on the assessor to determine which properties are eligible for agricultural use valuation. Any program that defines eligibility in terms of use presents this difficulty. It forces the assessor to go beyond the technical matter of estimating value, to require him to distinguish between agricultural and nonagricultural use. It is, of course, not unusual for the assessor to be called on, as one step in his valuation process, to classify land according to use. This is a key part of any property description. But the purpose in classifying according to use is normally that of aiding the assessor in establishing an accurate estimate of market value. Under use-value assessment laws the objective is the opposite. Here the intent is to select out properties to which a different concept of value is to be applied, a concept that may produce (indeed, is so designed) a quite different result in terms of assessed value.

It is generally accepted, I believe, that administrative problems are created when the assessor is placed in the position of going beyond the technical job of estimating the value of property. For example when, under fractional assessment, he becomes in effect a budget officer, he takes on responsibilities that were never intended to be his and that he cannot discharge properly. When, as is required under the old-age property tax exemptions of many states, he must determine how old the taxpayer is, whether he in fact lives in the house for which exemption is claimed, and how much income he and all other members of the household have, the assessor takes on the role of a social worker. When he is asked to ascertain which properties qualify for preferential tax treatment and which do not, he is made to function as a land-use planner.

It is, in my opinion, a grave weakness in most use-value assessment laws that they place the assessor, whose job is at best a difficult and sensitive one, in the position of deciding between eligible and ineligible properties—a distinction on which many tax dollars may depend and which may affect the pattern of urban development. It is inherent in any program that gives something away that such distinctions be made. I am not certain which officer of local government should be responsible for drawing this distinction; I am quite sure the assessor is not the best man for this job.

I have argued that there exists a genuine problem of tax equity and of tax administration in applying the property tax in its raw form to undeveloped land in urban-fringe areas. However, the remedy commonly employed (preferential assessment for land used in agriculture) raises as many problems of equity and administration as it solves. I turn therefore to the question whether there is a better way to deal with assessment of this troublesome category of property.

In states and communities where the principle of community control over land use has gained acceptance, it seems to me that tax relief for urban-fringe land is a natural by-product of the community's effort to discourage or prevent development in certain parts of the countryside. Implementation of a land-use control program involves the owner's giving up some of the rights in his land. These rights may be severed, as is the case when development rights are sold or given to a public body, or they may merely be held in abeyance, as is the case under agricultural or large-lot zoning. In either case, there is a restriction on use of the land, which presumably influences its market value and hence its assessment. The *ad valorem* principle would seem to be fully applicable here and would produce tax relief in proportion to the restrictions the owner accepted on use of his land.

There would, of course, still be certain administrative difficulties. Valuation of tracts from which certain rights had been severed would pose problems, at least until sufficient time had elapsed for a number of such properties to be sold. On the other hand, there is a distinct administrative advantage in the assessor's being able to shoot at a relatively unambiguous target and in his being relieved of the necessity to pass judgment on the eligibility of particular properties or property owners for tax abatement.

In states or communities that have not adopted plans for land use and control of development, preferential assessment cannot be supported as a method of shaping the pattern of development. As I have indicated, tax abatement alone can contribute little or nothing to a socially desirable pattern of land use.

In such areas, the case for tax relief to urban-fringe properties must rest on equity grounds. In my opinion this case can be made. But I would argue strongly that any tax relief not associated with restrictions on land use should take the form of a *deferral* rather than outright reduction in assessment. The essential feature of a tax deferral is that it gives nothing away. It is therefore appropriate in a situation in which the landowner sacrifices nothing of his freedom to use his land in any way he wants.

The farmer or other owner whose income is so limited that his rising taxes place a serious burden on him would thus pay little or even no tax until his property is sold or developed, at which time the back taxes would become due, with interest. A further advantage of this approach is that it enables the assessor more readily to apply a market assessment to this property, without feeling that in doing so he is forcing the poor owner off his land.

One criticism of the tax deferral is that it requires a dual assessment on the land—one an *ad valorem* assessment, on which the full tax is based, and the other a lower assessment representing only the "agricultural value," on which the farmer-owner is taxed currently. The deferral is said thus to double the assessor's work. However, as long as the deferral provides for full recapture of all deferred taxes, with interest, there is little reason to be concerned with the accuracy of the agricultural-value assessment. Indeed, there is no compelling reason for not deferring the entire tax. One great advantage of a plan that offers tax relief without actually giving anything away is that it simplifies the job of determining who is eligible and for how much.

The problem remains, however, of establishing an accurate *ad valorem* assessment. As indicated above, there are formidable obstacles to doing so with the usual assessment techniques.

Perhaps a solution might be found in some alternative

method of taxation that would exact about the same amount of tax, but would avoid the problem of valuation. Suggestions have been made, for example, to tax land in transition zones at the time it sells, on the basis of the gain in value since the last sale and the length of time that has elapsed since then. Another proposal would base the tax on the differences between the assessed value and the sale price. Of course, such approaches raise administrative problems of their own that may be no less irksome than those they are intended to avoid. Moreover, these alternatives must produce a result, in terms of tax due, that conforms closely to that obtained from the conventional approach, if we are to avoid the troublesome administrative and equity problem of distinguishing between eligible and ineligible properties.

Unless some workable plan can be devised to substitute for the *ad valorem* taxation of fringe land—a prospect that stirs little optimism—I see no escape from the necessity of devoting intensified effort along conventional lines to the job of establishing and maintaining accurate assessments on such properties. Principal reliance must inevitably be placed on sale-price data, deceptive though they may often be. If this is to be done, it is urgent that better guidelines be developed for interpreting and applying sale-price data in this segment of the land market. With urban influences becoming increasingly pervasive in the market for undeveloped land, this task should receive high priority from both theorists and property tax administrators.

Note

1 United States Department of Agriculture, *Selected Legislative and Other Documents on the Preferential Assessment of Farmland* (Economic Research Service, March, 1963) ; Council of State Governments (with cooperation of the International Association of Assessors Office), *Farm Land Assessment Practices in the United States* (August, 1966) .

Henry Aaron

Some Observations on Property Tax Valuation and the Significance of Full Value Assessment

The property tax has been reviled for decades as bad in principle and worse in practice. It is not well correlated with ability to pay or with the incidence of benefits from government services. It is poorly administered, more poorly without question than any other major tax. But predictions of the demise of the property tax have proved premature. In fact, renewed interest in and hope for reform of the property tax are both at higher levels than they have been for many years. Major scholarly work has suggested that past condemnations of the property tax in principle may have been somewhat overdrawn.[1] The first real hope for improved administration has been given us by a succession of recent court decisions attacking unequal assessments. And a number of compensatory changes in nonproperty taxes, specifically through such measures as the tax credit for the aged that was adopted in Wisconsin, give some hope that the most egregious vertical inequities of the property tax may be countered. All of this, ironically, is occurring against a background of proposals for federal-state revenue sharing—block grants or personal income tax credits —which offer the prospect that state and local reliance on property taxes can be reduced. There is a very real chance that, after living for years with a property tax, attacked for its quite real faults but accepted because nothing better was available, we may now be on the verge of reforming the property tax, only to see its relative importance decline sharply.

Whatever the future relative importance of the property tax, its absolute significance is bound to remain great. The reform in administration which the courts have set in motion is therefore of considerable importance. In my discussion of this reform, I should like to try to distinguish analytically the technical or economic facets from the political aspects of property tax administration, although a distinction is neither real nor altogether possible. I shall touch on three general areas. First, what are appraisers trying to measure? Second, is it full value or equal value assessments that we really want? Third, how can we use appraising resources most effectively to achieve full or equal value assessments?

What Are Appraisers Trying to Measure?

The answer quite simply is that there is no precise answer. The various valuation techniques yield different, sometimes widely different, results. In some cases most of us could agree about which valuation technique seems most reasonable. But more often there would be a range of disagreement of perhaps 10 percent, plus or minus, concerning what the "true value" of property really is. But the very locution, "true value," is misleading, for in fact there is no such thing.

Not since the Middle Ages have any reputable thinkers about economic matters contended that any object has a "true," "just," "fair," or any other kind of value besides that which people are prepared to pay for it in the market. Yet, for reasons with which we all are quite familiar, actual selling prices are an unsatisfactory base against which to levy property tax rates. So instead we must turn to one or another appraisal technique. But what do we wish to construct with that technique?

To answer that question, let me propose an imaginary world in which the market for real property differs from the one we know in only one respect: each parcel of real property is sold at least once a year. All of the other peculiarities which affect selling prices also exist in this imaginary world—pride of ownership and fluctuating credit conditions, for example—so that a given buyer-seller couple may agree upon a widely different selling price from the one upon which another buyer-seller couple would agree. The question I should like to pose is this: in such a world, would we use any other base for the real property tax than actual market prices? Although there is room for disagreement, the answer, I think, is that we would use selling price, not replacement cost less depreciation, not capitalized rents, or any other indirect method. We would recognize that price is affected by special considerations. But so, for example, is the income of a man who values highly the community in which he lives and therefore is content to earn considerably less than he could earn elsewhere. As we make no attempt to measure the psychic income from having good neighbors under the personal income tax, so we would not attempt to measure the psychic income of pride of ownership under the real property tax. We would probably also ignore the value of a favorable transferrable mortgage, since the attempt to value only one kind of intangible property would be altogether arbitrary. We would recognize that any attempt to go beyond the valuation of the market would be fraught with the risk of arbitrariness and inequities.

The preceding argument leaves one plausible reason for the use of valuation standards other than market price, and that is the fact that most real property is not sold sufficiently often. As a result, changing prices rapidly make old market prices inaccurate and inequitable indicators of current value. Moreover, even if market prices did not change, special factors which influence selling prices would have to be carried on the property tax rolls for long times. In practice, property taxes cannot be assessed on the basis of market prices. However, the foregoing argument does suggest that current selling prices should be used to the greatest extent possible in appraising property for tax purposes, a point which I shall expand below. It suggests further that the purpose of appraisal is to estimate values which *on the average* will equal actual selling prices. Since we can observe selling prices only sporadically and we have no, or very little, idea in which specific cases the special factors will appear that cause property values to deviate from our sense of the average, appraisers must adopt techniques which reach the right answer only on the average and cannot be expected to do so in every case.

Do We Want Full Value or Equal Value Assessments?

It is a truism that assessment at full value is mathematically irrelevant to equitable distribution of property tax burdens within a single jurisdiction. If each property is assessed at full value, than at some rate, r, the tax will yield the same revenue as if each property were assessed at some fraction, f, of full value and the rate were r/f. In a purely technical sense, equal value assessments are all that matter, since, if all properties are assessed at the same fraction of true value, the tax burden on each property depends only on the total amount of revenue collected.

In fact, this arithmetic is so obvious and beyond dispute that one seems to be driven immediately to the conclusion that the choice between full and fractional value assessments is of interest only as the choice affects the ease or difficulty with which equal value assessments can be achieved. These appear not to be separate issues at all. The question I have just posed should be rephrased to read, "Do we need full value assessments in order to get equal value assessments?" The answer, at this point, is far from clear, because until very recently most jurisdictions neither attempted to assess real property at or near full value nor took steps which would have facilitated equal value assessments at substantially less than full value.

To achieve equal value assessments in the absence of a full value standard requires full disclosure of whatever standard is in use and a refined appeal procedure, along the lines advocated by John Shannon.[2] Full disclosure increases the likelihood that fractional value assessments are also equal value assessments. To my knowledge, few, if any, property tax jurisdictions follow such a full disclosure policy. There can be no question that full disclosure, even under a fractional standard, would lead to the end of the most egregiously unequal assessments. At the same time, one may suspect that taxpayers will react more vigorously to assessment at, say, 120 percent under a full value standard than they would to assessment at, say, 24 percent under a 20 percent standard, even though our mathematical truism tells us that the relative overassessment in the two cases is identical. It seems likely that full value assessments will increase the effectiveness of any sincere efforts to promote equal value assessments by encouraging taxpayer participation in the assessing process.

There is a quite independent reason why full value assessments are beneficial, a reason which is unrelated to the desirability of equitable sharing of property tax burdens. Full value assessment on all properties, readily available to the public, are an extremely valuable form of information. First, they are valuable to policymakers who can then easily observe the real burden of taxes and apply exemptions with an accurate understanding of their consequences. Second, they are valuable to banks and other appraisers whose job can be materially shortened and cheapened by accurate municipal assessments. Third, they are valuable to redevelopment authorities, to city planners, and to private builders for whom trends in property values can be immensely useful in planning the provision of new urban services, the construction of new improvements, rezoning, and the development of long-range plans.[3]

Consider, for example, a question about where an urban renewal project should be assigned. In most communities there is today no comprehensive and reliable measure by which decision makers can determine the amount of urban blight, the speed of its advance, and the exceptions to urban blight. As redevelopment policy moves toward selective, rather than wholesale, renewal of declining areas, our need to study trends and patterns and, perhaps, infer causes of "the life and death of great American cities" will become increasingly important.

I am not suggesting that full value assessments will be the decisive input into this decision process, nor am I arguing that completely equal fractional assessments could not also be of use. But I am urging that widely available data on trends in property values, readily usable without prior processing, can be of material assistance to wide segments of the population and to decision makers. Just as one could not contemplate rational fiscal policy before the development of comprehensive national income account statistics, so also the job of building and rebuilding our cities is hindered by the lack of good, comprehensive information on what the market says they are worth.

This brings me to the issue of what, indeed, has been happening in full value assessment. Ten years ago the answer would have been simple—almost nothing. Even six years ago there were only eight major property tax jurisdictions, with an aggregate population of just under 800,000, in which at least half of nonfarm single-family residences were assessed at 70 percent or more of value.[4] In only nine, with a total population of 1,100,000, was the coefficient of dispersion less than .1, indicating that appraisals differed from selling prices by less then 10 percent on the average, a reasonable target for equal assessments.[5] These figures contrast sharply with the fact that twenty-five states today have laws requiring full value assessments.[6] However, twenty-nine states required full value assessments in 1965. Since then California, Michigan, Ohio, and Rhode Island have explicitly renounced the statewide requirement of full value assessment. In one state (California), a case now in the courts may compel a return to full value assessment — full value in fact, not just in law. The repeal of the full value standard in Rhode Island, with replacement by a local option rule, is particularly disappointing in view of the fact that two of Rhode Island's four major jurisdictions, including Providence, already exceeded the 70 percent standard, used earlier.

The growing unwillingness of the courts to tolerate tacit assessment standards, usually badly administered, which are inconsistent with state constitutional or legal standards, has driven state legislatures in two directions. On the one hand, some states, such as the four just mentioned, have adopted explicit fractional standards with which they felt assessors could live. In a number of others, such as Massachusetts, Florida, and Kentucky, there have been local or statewide moves to honor constitutional provisions calling for full value assessments. It is too early to determine which trend, if either, will predominate. For the first time in decades, however, there is hope that property tax administration will not be indisputably worse than that of any major tax. If this direction continues, we will have the courts to thank for shouldering yet another task which the executive or legislative organs of government seemed unable or unwilling to face.

How Can We Use Appraisal Resources Most Efficiently?

The courts may set us on the path to more accurate and more equitable assessments, but it will be by the sweat of the appraiser's brow and the courage of state and local politicians that good property tax administration will be sustained.[7] Yet today many property tax jurisdictions use their appraisers with considerable inefficiency, and few or no jurisdictions allocate the efforts of their appraisers in a genuinely scientific manner.

There is a basic question here: if we assume that assessors desire to make equal full value appraisals, that they have the political support to do so, and that they are willing to engage in a full disclosure policy, such as that described previously, how can they allocate scarce and costly appraising talent most efficiently in order to attain equitable assessments?

The economists here should immediately recognize that this problem is really a standard production function problem of the kind normally treated in the first year of graduate school. Each jurisdiction has a given level of appraising resources which can be increased at some cost. There is some unique way by which it can allocate its stock of appraisers' efforts so as to maximize their output, and, if we are willing to assign some value to the output of appraisers, there is a unique and determinable level of public expenditures at which the marginal productivity of appraisers' services will just equal their marginal cost. For the purposes of the following discussion, I shall assume that our goal is to produce the most equitable possible assessments as measured by some indicator of dispersion around the average assessment-sales ratio.

To explain how the efforts of appraisers should be allocated, I shall once again begin with an unrealistically simple world in which the tasks of the appraisers are so simple they do not even exist. Then, by adding elements of reality, we will see how the talents of appraisers should be allocated in order to maximize the efficiency of their efforts, that is, to achieve an assessment-sales ratio around which there is minimum dispersion.[8]

First, let us assume that all property values remain absolutely stable from year to year. In such a world, appraisers need value properties only once; their job is then entirely done. We can ascertain stability by comparing original appraisals with sales prices; by assumption the relation between them will not change.

The employment prospects for appraisers would be no better if all property values changed each year by a uniform percentage. In this case, as before, all properties would have to be valued only once. Thenceforth, all values could be altered by whatever uniform percentage change in value was revealed by sales prices. In fact, the equitable allocation of property taxes would not require such multiplication, since each property would constitute the same portion of the tax base before as after multiplication.

These oversimplified examples should suffice to drive home a point that will have been obvious to most—that *the services of appraisers are needed, not because property values change, but because they change by differing proportions.*

Now let us assume that there are two kinds of property. Each year Type 1 property changes in value by an average of *x* percent per year, and Type 2 property changes in value by an average of *y* percent per year. But these are only averages. The value of some Type 1 properties changes by more, and that of some by less, than *x* percent. The same is true of Type 2 property. In this case the assessor has a problem. He can estimate the change in a property's value by ascertaining whether it is

Type 1 or Type 2, but he will be right only on the average. If the range of changes in value of each type of property is small, say, plus or minus 10 percent of the average change in value, then his estimate will be accurate enough for tax purposes. Thus, if the average change in value of Type 1 property is, say, 20 percent, but some properties change in value by 18 percent and others by 22 percent, no one will much criticize the assessor if he increases the assessments of all properties by 20 percent (or 18 percent, if he wants to be on the safe side). On the other hand, if the distribution of the changes in value of a certain type of property is very wide, then statistical estimates can get the assessor in trouble; on-the-spot appraisals will be necessary to determine at which end of the scale the change in value of a particular property falls. Thus, if the average change in Type 2 property is 5 percent, but the value of many properties changed not at all, or declined, while the value of many others increased by 10 percent or more, a blanket 5 percent increase in assessments of Type 2 properties will produce serious inequities and much litigation.

If the assessor cannot reappraise each property every year, it is clear that appraising resources should be concentrated on those kinds of properties whose values are changing at different rates, in this case on Type 2 property. Only one qualification is necessary. If valuation of Type 2 property is extremely costly, in the sense that each appraisal takes a great deal of time relative to appraisal of Type 1 property, then this judgment may have to be modified.

If we leave the world of abstraction and return to the world of practical problems, where valuation is imprecise, the valuation of different kinds of property cannot be neatly categorized, and countless other imperfections exist, then does the abstract proposition hold up—that appraisal resources should be concentrated on those types of property with most divergent value changes? The answer is that it holds up moderately well. I should like to describe the prescription for allocation of appraising effort to which it leads. It will turn out, I think, that the prescription will resemble rule-of-thumb procedures in use in the more advanced property tax jurisdictions.[9]

In step 1 an assessment-sales ratio study is undertaken based on the most recent data available for a twelve-month period. Data of questionable accuracy or on sales not believed to be at arm's length are excluded. The remaining observations are stratified by region, type of property, value of property, age of improvements, *or any other set of variables* which, it is felt, will produce categories as nearly homogeneous as possible with respect to the proportional change in property values, as measured by assessment-sales ratios. The choice of variables to be used in stratifying observations is a matter of judgment and experience, not theory. The selection depends on whatever factors may be influencing property values in a given community.

In step 2 the assessor estimates the average cost in appraisers' time necessary to revalue each type of property and the number of appeals which he feels the appeal process can handle.

In step 3 the assessor must articulate the relative importance he attaches to incorrect assessments of various kinds. Is he equally concerned about all undervaluations of 30 percent, regardless of which subclassification of property is involved (i.e., regardless of location, price, use, etc.), or is he equally concerned by all undertaxation of a given absolute amount, regardless of which subclassification of property is involved? Does his concern about incorrect assessment rise in proportion to the absolute amount of error, in proportion to the square of the error, or in some more complex fashion? Through this process the assessor would declare explicitly what his practices now declare implicitly—how important he considers various inequities to be.

With these three kinds of information—distributions of assessment-sales ratios on relatively homogeneous property classes, the cost of appraising property in such classes, and the value judgments which an assessor must apply—it would be a relatively simple matter to calculate how appraising resources should be allocated to maximize the efficiency with which they are used.

It is, of course, impossible to describe, in the abstract, what concrete recommendations would flow from such an analysis. The results would depend on the frequency and typicalness of sales, the cost and skill of appraisers, and, most importantly, the value judgments of assessors. A few general observations can be made in advance, however.

First, large classes of property could be revalued annually on the basis of sales data with little, if any, actual appraising. These properties would be members of categories for which assessment-sales ratios were tightly bunched around the observed average. This procedure of "mass," or "block," reassessment is already used in some of the more advanced property tax jurisdictions.

Second, appraising resources would be concentrated on those classes of property for which assessment-sales ratios were widely dispersed, the costs of appraisal and the value judgments of appraisers being taken into account. All properties in the categories where assessment-sales ratios exhibited greatest dispersion would be reappraised.

Third, the appeal process would become an integral part of the administrative process. Indeed, unless there is a significant number of appeals each year, it is likely that underassessments are excessively large. Those categories of properties that are statistically revalued, as mentioned first above, are bound to contain some specific properties the values of which have changed by widely different amounts from the average. Obviously, beyond some point it is cheaper to handle those relatively few cases through an appeal mechanism than it would be to appraise all properties in the category.

Fourth, certain rules of thumb would have to be retained. The appeals procedure will take care of overassessments among classes of property that will be statistically valued. But it will not take care of underassessments. Accordingly, there should be rules that each property will be reassessed no less often than every z years, where z is chosen on the basis of the trade-off on the returns from these appraisals as against the appraisals made on the basis of assessment-sales ratio studies. In general, z will be different for different types of property. For example, it is conceivable that commercial property on a developing urban fringe should be appraised on the spot no less often than, say, every two years, whereas property in a stable residential community would require on-the-spot appraisal no more often than every fifteen years. Another rule of thumb that should probably be retained is reappraisal of properties for which improvement licenses have been granted, although here, again, statistical methods may be called for. On the other hand, the rule that property should be appraised whenever sold should be dropped, although this judgment might have to be qualified if the availability of data on sales prices materially shortened the amount of time it took to appraise such properties.

Fifth, some categories will have so few sales that no statistical inferences may be drawn from assessment-sales ratio information. There are three possible ways out. Sales over a longer period may be studied and, through the inclusion of more observations, statistical significance obtained; this approach has the obvious drawback that the older sales will tend to be unrepresentative of current market conditions. The second approach is to estimate the dispersion on the basis of those of similar categories for which inferences can be drawn. Finally, such properties may be appraised. This alternative is to be avoided if possible because it is costly in terms of the scarce resource, appraisers' time.

Sixth, the fact that this whole approach obviously depends on the existence of reliable and extensive information on selling prices suggests that information should be collected on sales, and data on revenue stamps should be gathered wherever they are not now collected. It also suggests that this method will yield greatest returns in large jurisdictions and will be of little or no use in very small towns or rural areas.

All of this may sound rather complex. Mathematically, it is quite simple. The techniques described here are similar to those used with spectacular success in cost-effectiveness studies in the Defense Department and to those used by the Internal Revenue Service in determining which income tax returns to audit. Far from reducing the role or significance of the assessor or the appraiser, this technique would aid him in doing an expert job as efficiently as possible. Such performance is possible, of course, only when the property tax office enjoys reasonable political support or, as we have been learning of late, if the courts take an active interest in property tax administration.

As one distinguished property tax administrator remarked, constitutional requirements for full value assessment have meant that the office of assessor is the only one for which perjury has been a condition for office. The courts are calling on us to abolish the condition. I have suggested that it is also economically desirable that we do so and that we adopt scientific methods for carrying out new assessment procedures as cheaply as possible.

Notes

1 Dick Netzer, *Economics of the Property Tax* (Washington, D.C.: Brookings Institution, 1966) .

2 John Shannon, "Full Disclosure Policy—The State's Role in the Assessment Process," presented at the Tax Institute of America Symposium, November 2, 1966, Chicago, Illinois. Shannon's full disclosure policy consists of four prescriptions: (1) annual assessment ratio studies; (2) wide publicity for the results; (3) legislation stipulating that assessment ratios resulting from these studies may be introduced by taxpayers in appeals; (4) establishment of a tolerance zone to make full disclosure tolerable for assessment officials.

Under the second condition Shannon stated, "Frankly, I hope the day will come when all property tax bills carry the following notation: 'Based on assessment ratio studies made by the State tax department, property in your district is being assessed generally at [—— percent] of current market value. If you believe that the assessed valuation on your property is not in line with the prevailing assessment level, contact the [county clerk's office] for information concerning the time and place for registering an assessment appeal.' "

In the day of the computer, one need not stop here. It would be quite simple to insert the following additions between the foregoing two sentences: "Your property has been assessed at [$——]. This assessment implies that your property has a market value of [$——]."

3 In a telephone conversation on May 22, 1967, Richard Chandler, Assessor of Richmond, one of the few jurisdictions in which assessments are close to full value, confirmed that the property tax rolls are extensively used by private appraisers and real estate developers for the purposes set forth in the text.

4 United States Bureau of the Census, *Census of Governments:*

Taxable Property Values, 1962 (Washington, D.C.: U.S. Government Printing Office, 1963), II, Table 22. The jurisdictions were Greenwich, Connecticut; Manatee, Florida; Seminole, Florida; Montgomery, New York; Providence, Rhode Island; Warwick, Rhode Island; Richmond, Virginia; Green Bay, Wisconsin.

5 The jurisdictions were Greenwich, Connecticut; New Britain, Connecticut; West Hartford, Connecticut; Kent, Delaware; Montgomery, Maryland; Washington, Maryland; Sumter, South Carolina; Fairfax, Virginia; Green Bay, Wisconsin: *Census of Governments*, II, Table 22.

6 John Shannon, "Full Disclosure Policy," Appendix A.

7 In this regard the paper of James E. Luckett, "Experiment in Democracy," presented at National Tax Association Conference, September 27, 1966, Denver, Colorado, should be "must" reading. Luckett reports the generally smooth transition from fractional to full value assessments despite initial skepticism on the part of citizens and tax administrators.

8 I shall intentionally leave the measure of dispersion unspecified. The measure of dispersion incorporates value judgments about the relative undesirability of assessments which deviate from the average by different amounts. For example, the "coefficient of dispersion" implies that underassessment and overassessment are equally undesirable. It implies also that there is no reason to choose between the situation in which one property is underassessed twenty percent, while another property is correctly assessed, and another situation in which two properties are both underassessed ten percent. These value judgments may be right or wrong, but they should be made explicit. I suspect that a measure of dispersion which accurately showed the preferences of assessors, of city governments, or of taxpayers would be a good deal more complex than the "coefficient of dispersion."

9 In fact, the procedure described here resembles that described by Ronald B. Welch, "Maintenance of Appraisals," presented at 10th Annual Conference of the Western States Association of Tax Administrators, October 4, 1961, Sun Valley, Idaho. The proposal presented in my text above involves considerably more statistical analysis. But practical considerations might cause the final product not to differ by much from California practice in many instances.

10 *A. M. Woodruff*

Assessment Standards: Highest and Best Use as a Basis for Land Appraisal and Assessment

The concept of "highest and best use"—that use which yields the optimum return—comes up, in connection with assessing, chiefly during arguments concerning which assessment base would be most appropriate. (Since the words "highest and best use" appear repeatedly in this paper, they are abbreviated hereafter to "HBU.") The HBU concept must be related to market value, and in most cases the value justified by HBU coincides with that recognized by the market. In a monomodal market this could hardly be otherwise, but in a bimodal or trimodal market interesting deviations occur. Frequently, moreover, the HBU and the market value both exceed what influential taxpayers consider a reasonable basis for their assessments. They then argue eloquently, and recently with some political success, that some other base be recognized.

In transitional neighborhoods in cities and on the urban fringe, the feeling is general that *potential* HBU in the visible future will justify values far above those of the moment.[1] This anticipation leads to a game in which the bewildered former users are often shouldered aside, those who can eventually use the property for its potential HBU wait patiently for the opportune moment, and the intervening owners play more or less frantically, guessing when that moment will come. While the owners delay sale to maximize their profits, they wish to minimize their taxes, and their own aspirations become entangled in conflicting concepts of what constitutes good city planning. The question remains: if they receive temporary tax forgiveness, should they be asked to repay all or part of what has been forgiven when their profits materialize?

The Concept of Market Value

The mission of the appraiser or assessor, and for present purposes they are interchangeable, is to find market value. The terms in which the courts have defined market value may be paraphrased as the price which a willing buyer would pay and a willing seller accept, provided each was fully informed, had adequate time to negotiate, and was free from any unusual pressure. The verbal embroidery varies among court decisions, but the substance of the definition is fairly standard. An economic semanticist would observe that this is a definition of price rather than of value, but that is a distinction which need not be debated here.

To the standard definition most economists would add the word "average" to describe both the buyer and the seller in question. The figure representing HBU generally coincides with the figure representing the consensus of willing and informed buyers and sellers. After all, if the parties are both willing and informed, they may be assumed to know what the highest and best use is; and, if they do, why would a seller take less than the HBU price?

Behavior of the Exceptional Buyer or Seller in a Near-Ideal Market

The behavior of the cases at the extremities of the supply and demand curves is of particular interest. In Figure 10.1, *D* is a potential buyer who does not have to buy, but who drives about the city making offers on parcel after parcel at figures that informed sellers will not accept. He enjoys the sport, is pleased with himself, and is cordially loathed by all real estate brokers. Every once in a while, however, D meets C, a nonaverage seller who is not well informed and who must sell quickly. A sale takes place, between two atypical individuals.

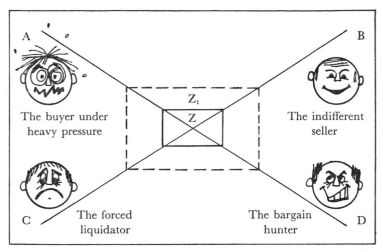

Figure 10.1.—The attitudes of various participants in a market for reasonably homogeneous property.

At the other extremity, B personifies many property owners who put a price on their property above any expectation of immediate sale, but hope some day to get it. A, on the other hand, is a man in trouble; perhaps he has just come to town, his wife is sick, his mother-in-law is ailing, the children have mumps, and his new boss is very demanding. In short, he has to have a house, and immediacy is more important than price. If he meets B, a sale may take place at a relatively high price.

The fact that A needs a house badly, and is willing to pay more for it than would average buyers, does not of itself mean that the HBU of all houses is to accommodate necessitous buyers. The HBU is to accommodate the average, and the exceptional buyer who ignores the average price and pays more than necessary establishes empirically only the imperfection of the market.

Meanwhile at point Z, numerous informed buyers and sellers are meeting and making deals. These are the market participants who are both average and willing. B is nonaverage since he is a reluctant seller, and A and C are under duress and hence nonaverage. This nonaverage behavior does not alter the fact that HBU and average market value generally coincide.

The Zone of Consensus

It may be assumed that the market consists of buyers-sellers, some eager, some in distress, some reluctant, and some euphoric. The structure of the market ordains that they do not move at random as do gas atoms within an enclosure, but that they tend to cluster around point Z where most of the sales occur.

For convenience we can call the small box at Z the zone of market consensus. The size of Z is a function of the homogeneity of the article traded, the availability of market data, and the mobility of market participants. The assumptions might indicate that no sales should occur outside Z because each buyer should find out on his shopping tour what is happening at Z, and, having found out, he would pay no more, while no seller would accept less. The facts are otherwise, and experience has shown that, even under near-ideal conditions, a small number, say, about 2 percent, of the transactions occur outside Z. Under these conditions the appraiser, following the uniformly accepted assumption that the next sale will not depart much from the level established by the last one, has about a 98 percent chance of predicting the next sale with substantial correctness.

This model fits only near-ideal conditions, such as the market for tract houses or row houses, which are all very much alike. If the model is altered to fit the market for unusual houses, the zone of consensus reflects the difficulty of comparison, or, in other words, the lack of homogeneity of the items traded; and Z in Figure 10.1 spreads out to Z'.

Fair market value and HBU are identical in the cases described. These cases involved both reasonably homogeneous properties and reasonably homogeneous buyers and sellers. In other words, if a frequency distribution were made of the participants in this market, it would bear considerable resemblance to the bell-shaped curve, with a concentration in the middle around Z, and relatively few individuals at the tails.

The Case of the Bimodal or Trimodal Market for Industrial Property

In some complex market situations, bimodality or trimodality emerges among the market participants, and a frequency distribution would have either two or three maxima. This was dramatically demonstrated in the case of a public auction of a property which had been used as a sugar refinery. It had been closed for many years, but the machinery was intact and was operational. A trimodal market developed.

At the start of the auction, a group of bargain hunters exchanged bids up to about $100,000. When the bargain hunters' play was exhausted, they dropped out and the warehousemen took over. They in turn ran the price quickly to about $250,000. At this point a previously inconspicuous gentleman in a barely audible voice offered $400,000. The man beside him raised the bid to $800,000, and between them they inched the price up to $1,025,000. Each represented a sugar refinery which wanted the plant for its HBU, whereas the warehousemen wanted it for alternative uses. Had only one manufacturer been interested, however, he could have bought it for about $300,000, just enough to shut out the warehousemen.

Thus if only one HBU buyer is in circulation, the price settles at or near the level for alternative use. If two or more HBU buyers are in the market to bid against each other, the price moves up to the HBU level. This situation arises only with respect to property which is in some way specialized. The buyer who wants and can use the specialized feature can afford to pay accordingly, but he obviously will not do so unless he has to. If only one buyer who can use the specialized features is on hand, he is likely to get quite a windfall. This buyer is quite different from the "stray" in the normal market who pays too much for a standard item through either impatience or ignorance.

The sale at alternative use value, in this case $300,000, goes far toward establishing the level at which the property can be

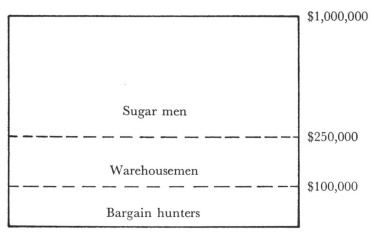

Figure 10.2.—A trimodal market for industrial property.

assessed for tax purposes. This is so because the wording of statutes and court decisions largely emphasizes that, if buyers and sellers, dealing at arm's length, agree on a consideration, this agreement becomes persuasive evidence of market value. When sales are few and far between, the occurrence of a single sale looms large. Industrial assessments are complex, not the least reason being the thinness of the market for industrial property and the likelihood that particular items will trade at variance from the figure which would represent HBU. Assessment of such property should be undertaken only by a qualified specialist, who can discriminate between HBU and off-beat sales on the one hand, and who can properly evaluate and allow for locational and functional obsolescence on the other.

The "Classic" Urban Under-user

The classic urban under-user differs from the cases previously described. The law generally is on the side of the assessor, but political pressures and possibly public sympathy may be against him. The typical case involves a single-family house, which, either by itself or in company with similar houses, is engulfed by changed and more profitable uses. The owner or owners cling stubbornly to their homes, but they could at any time sell for HBU. To complicate matters, the owners may come from the great "old families" with considerable political influence, or they may be relatively poor individuals who happen to want to stay in a location which is familiar to them but which others want for a more intensive use. In the one instance they may exert covert influence; in the other they may arouse overt sympathy.

City planners sometimes urge that volunatry under-use be eliminated so that it will not impede progress, and they may talk darkly of eminent domain and urban renewal to make the intransigent conform to their land use plans. The planners, on the other hand, may want to preserve the under-use for its aesthetic or historical value.

The market of an under-used property is established by its neighbors and closely approximates HBU value. The assessors' mechanical job is relatively easy, but, if the property is to be retained in planned under-use, some tax concession must be granted to make the continued under-use possible. Some Australian states give temporary relief to such under-users and also to owners of urban-fringe land not yet ripe for development. The temporary relief is generally contingent on owner occupancy, and, when the property is sold for another and more profitable use, it is generally subject to five years' retroactive taxes based on an assessment reflecting the HBU. Normally this tax is paid by the seller, but, whoever pays it, the point is that the municipality is in a position to collect it and be recompensed for the period of forbearance.

The Transitional Owner in Town

The transitional owner in town is still another case, similar to the classic urban under-user in that the owner is a candidate for a tax concession and frequently a lachrymose petitioner for favored treatment; but the transitional owner is quite unlike the classic urban under-user, since he cannot presently sell for what is probably a clearly visible but still *potential* HBU price.

Like the case described in an earlier section, this segment of the market is roughly trimodal. Its essential characteristic is the high probability that the property will be worth considerable money in the future for a use which is clearly foreseeable, but meanwhile its value reflects only part of the future potential. At any given moment the owner's optimal course of action may be to do nothing but wait for the time when the property "becomes ripe." The HBU price of any particular moment reflects the informed guesses of shrewd guessers as to the timing. The discrepancy is between present and future HBU.

Since this discussion must consider futures, the following illustration assumes a time span of fifteen years. (Obviously if the time span were extended, for instance, to a century, the potential HBU would get beyond the reach even of a fevered imagination.) An example within the fifteen-year time span would be a tenement house near the center of a northern city. It is being used as a tenement and can presumably continue in this use more or less indefinitely. As such, it has a well-established value of $5,000. Numerous tenement house owners are circulating, and the house could easily be sold for the $5000 figure. The house occupies a lot 25 feet by 100 feet that has a potential HBU based on its inclusion, together with others, in a site of a more extensive improvement. Elsewhere on the fringes of "downtown," operators have paid $5.00 per square foot for such property, a rate which in this case would amount to $12,500.

Because the potential HBU buyer, although a rare bird, is known to exist, the average seller has an inclination to hold out for more than the $5000 figure justified by the current use of the property. If the seller is lucky and is also blessed with a long life, an HBU buyer may in fact come to rest on his roof-tree. Meanwhile the value—that is, what a willing buyer and a willing seller would agree to—fluctuates in a shadow land of uncertainty as to when the parcel will "become ripe."

The discrepancy in this case is not between a present HBU higher than a present sale price or higher than what an influential taxpayer will endure in silence. It is between a *potential* HBU, which is expected to materialize sometime, and a *present* HBU that is much lower. The optimal course of action is to sit and wait for the potential to develop. Meanwhile the assessor must work from such data as are available to determine the *present* HBU, which is also the present market value.

Eventually a sizable profit may materialize between the HBU in year one and the HBU in year fifteen. When realized, it will be subject to the 25 percent federal capital gains tax. The profit in its entirety may accrue to the one patient owner, or a series of smaller profits may be shared by the group of successive owners. Some argue that, since the profit arises from the social pressure of a growing city, society should be a larger partner than is provided for by a capital gains tax that is limited to 25 percent and is frequently less than that.

Conversely, the owner often argues that his property tax during the transitional wait should not be based on a value that recognizes the future potential discounted to the present —that is, the market value that numerous buyers and sellers actually recognize. The owner wants to be taxed on the *status quo ante* value of $5000 and claims that he will be forced into bankruptcy at higher levels of taxation.

Still another thread of argument comes from some planners who feel that slums can be taxed out of existence. They argue that the property should be taxed forthwith on the basis of its eventual potential HBU value, in order to penalize the "slumlords." The debate between an owner who wants to hold on until he can make a higher profit and a planner, to whom the ownership of slum property is an anathema, can be quite emotional.

The assessor should stay out of this particular network of high voltage circuits, assess the property for what the market

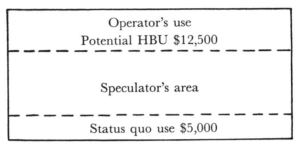

Figure 10.3.—A trimodal market for in-town transitional property.

indicates, review it frequently because the market changes erratically, and keep very well documented files. Needless to say, hopes rise and wane as the city seems first to be growing in one direction and then in another.

Transitional markets set up a guessing game, played for keeps by extremely shrewd players who are not known for their gentleness toward one another or toward the tax assessor. The professional guessers are the speculators who buy for more than the present use value in hopes of realizing on the potential HBU value. The assessor has to watch the guessing game closely and keep track of the guesses as they emerge in the form of consummated sales.

As mentioned before, this segment of the market is trimodal, the three modes being those shown in Figure 10.3.

The Transitional Owner on the Urban Fringe

The same general cast of characters plays the urban-fringe game. It is significant, on the other hand, that the owners of transitional fringe properties are often farmers, or at least pseudo-farmers, who can tap the reservoir of public sympathy generated by America's rural nostalgia. In contrast, the owners of transitional in-town properties often carry the tag of "slum-lord" and are held up to public obloquy. A frequency distribution of the participants in an urban-fringe market might look like Figure 10.4.

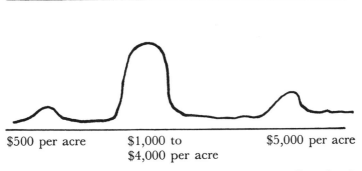

| $500 per acre | $1,000 to $4,000 per acre | $5,000 per acre |

Figure 10.4.—Frequency distribution of buyers-sellers in the urban-fringe market.

The urban-fringe guessing game is played for large prizes. A housing developer might pay, say, $5000 per acre for a tract which he considered ripe and which for farming would be worth, at a stretch, $500 an acre. Developers, however, almost never tie up their capital in land until they are ready to develop a tract, and hence they become active market participants only at the "last minute." They are sufficiently numerous, especially around large cities, to force each other to pay the HBU price. Enough profit lies between the $500 agricultural "floor" and the $5000 development "ceiling" to make the game exciting.

Whereas the speculator in the in-town transitional area is guessing whether the downtown part of the city will grow at all, the fringe speculator in the two decades since World War II has been betting on a sure thing, the only uncertainty being the timing. It has not always been so. At the end of the speculative 1920's, operators who had been winning such bets consistently for more than a decade suddenly found the odds changed. Their pecuniary losses were enormous, and so much land was taken over by cities for tax default that World War II came and went before the last of it was returned to private use.

The speculator performs the socially useful function of providing a market between the extremes, thus permitting an "original" owner, perhaps a bona fide farmer, to take part of the profit without having to wait out the whole transitional period and play "all or nothing." Often the speculator is also a partial user, in the sense that he uses the property to some extent for some purpose, such as light farming, during the interval between commercial farming and residential development. For his contribution in providing a market in the transitional interim the speculator certainly deserves some reward, but the forces which generate the eventual HBU value of $5000 per acre are created by society, and the public, therefore, is entitled to more than 25 percent of the prize. More will be said on this subject below.

The assessor, as usual, is in the middle. He is under pressure, on the one hand, to raise assessments as close as possible to eventual HBU, but, on the other, to hold them down to the *status quo ante* level supportable by farming. The interim owners are constantly complaining that the level of taxes makes it hard for them to hold on.

The planners have conflicting viewpoints. The words "urban open space" carry a pleasant sound; "urban sprawl" receives disapprobation. Keeping fringe land out of development produces both simultaneously. The appeal of the idea of urban open space has led some sixteen states to adopt legislation permitting an owner of urban-fringe land to choose to be taxed on agricultural-use value rather than any other value. Sensibly administered, such a policy should carry two kinds of restrictions: (1) the land must be kept in "green use," and (2) upon sale for a more profitable use, there should be provision to recapture the taxes which the public has forgone the while. Some of the present statutes provide for restrictions and sanctions for noncompliance; others do not.

Tax recovery can be either according to five-year retroactive taxation based on eventual HBU value, as in Australia, or according to a year-by-year computation of the dollars of tax forgiven between the agricultural value and the value of that year. The accumulated forgiveness is then subject to full or partial recapture at the time of sale, and constitutes a lien on the land until paid. In many ways it operates like a capital gains tax.

The contrary argument holds that the land should be forced into use, or at least into availability, by taxing it up to the allowable hilt. The reasoning is that this would force a lot of land onto the market at once and drive down the price. The geometry involved in this suggestion, however, is not comforting. Fringe land rather obviously is on the fringe, and each of a series of concentric circles (as in Figure 10.5) is much larger

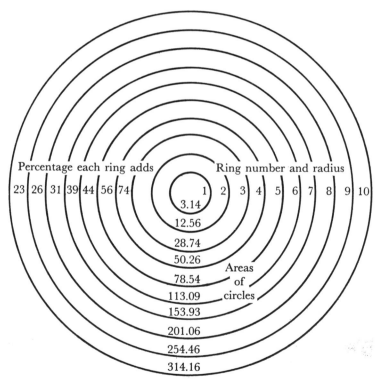

Figure 10.5.—Increment in land area produced by each acquisition of fringe land.

than the one next inside. If the radius of each larger circle is one unit (inch, foot, furlong, or mile, it makes no difference) greater than the radius of the circle inside it, the area of the tenth ring is equal to 23 percent of the total of the areas of rings one through nine. A "ring" around the outside of a city involves a great deal of land which can be used for farming, for pseudo-farming like gentlemen's small rural retreats, or for development. Seldom can a sizable ring be used for development all at once because seldom does a city grow that fast. Hence there is unlikely to be a development market on which it could all be forced.

The Australian procedure merits attention. Zoning is quite tight, so that on a metropolitan basis, not a local tax basis, fringe land becomes available only as it is needed. The zoning ordinances must be coupled with tax laws that grant concessions for those whose land is zoned "rural," and that include a recapture clause with real teeth in it. This procedure would prevent the leap-frogging at the edge of town so characteristic of the edges of American cities.

All these schemes make the assessor find a value for the property involved in the concession area on some basis other than its present market and *present* HBU value. It will be remembered that the *potential* HBU comes only in the future and is another problem. Assessing below present HBU is a nuisance because of the lack of data on which to base estimates, and experience has pointed out with painful clarity that the lack of data generally favors the owner against the assessor. In other words, in the absence of data to the contrary, appellate bodies often reduce assessments to the point where they encounter rock-hard data.

Capital Gains Taxation of the Unearned Increment

Any scheme for assessing substantially below present HBU almost certainly sets up sizable profits for the owner. Indeed, the low interim taxes almost constitute a license for the owner to play a tougher game of "hold-out" with larger profits at the end. Hence some form of profit recapture is necessary.

A scheme with much to recommend it was introduced by the Germans into their colony in Tsing-tao, Shantung Province, on the coast of mainland China in the late 1890's. This scheme imposed a capital gains tax at a steeply progressive rate on land profits. The same idea has been used on Taiwan by the government of the Republic of China. The tax rises from 20 percent on the increment of profit between 100 percent and 200 percent to 80 percent on the increment involved in the third doubling of the starting price (see Table 10.1). This tax

TABLE 10.1

CAPITAL GAINS TAX RATE SCHEDULE IN TAIWAN

Initial purchase price	Sale price	Profit (%)	Tax rate (%)	Tax dollars
100	200	100	20	20
	300	200	40	40
	400	300	60	60
	500	400	80	80
			TOTAL	200

rate schedule leaves a diminishing net profit through a five-fold increase in value, but recaptures all of the profit above that level.

It has often been pointed out that a capital gains tax large enough to recapture a significant part of the unearned increment would induce escape through the mechanism of lease-hold, which would defer for a long time the moment when the increment would be measured. This hole can be plugged with an automatic quinquennial revaluation, so that the capital gains are recomputed at these intervals. Obviously any such system must contain safeguards, lest the owner be taxed on price increases resulting from inflation. It must make due allowance also for all improvements which the owner made and paid for.

Summary

Generally market value and the value justified by highest and best use coincide closely or are in fact identical. While exceptional sales occur in near-ideal markets, these are not situations in which HBU and market value diverge. On the other hand, in a market which is bimodal or trimodal, the value justified by present or potential HBU and the market value of the moment may diverge. In the market for industrial property, an identifiable HBU value may be out of reach of the assessor, especially as concerns specialized property which only one buyer desires for its specialized use.

The "classic" urban under-user, the owner of transitional in-town property, and the owner of transitional fringe property all clamor for preferential assessment under present HBU, so that they can hold onto a property more comfortably to realize a developing potential and much higher HBU. If legislation requires the assessor to accommodate this demand, he must find a nonmarket-based value, a technically difficult undertaking.

Very large profits accrue through the ripening of transitional land, whether in town or on the fringe, to a new HBU. Society generates these profits, and a persuasive argument can be made that society should share in them to an extent greater than the 25 percent capital gains tax. If the owner or a sequence of owners has also had the benefit of preferential taxes based on a value below the present market value during the waiting period, the argument for public recapture of a larger share of the profit is even more persuasive.

Acknowledgments

The author gratefully acknowledges suggestions and criticism from Laszlo Ecker-Racz, recently of the United States Advisory Commission on Intergovernmental Relations, from Ronald Welch, Assistant Executive Secretary of the California State Tax Equalization Board, from Paul Corusy of the International Association of Assessing Officers, and from Anthony G. Ferraro of the Colorado State Tax Commission.

Note

1 "Potential HBU" is sometimes defined as a *use program,* a phrase meaning that what is HBU today is not going to be HBU tomorrow. The essential dynamism of the real estate market introduces an inevitable imprecision into the concept of potential HBU, since a series of uses lies in the future.

IV. ADMINISTRATION
   AND EVOLVING
   PROPERTY TAX POLICY

11 Shelley M. Mark

Property Tax Administration and Hawaii's Land Use Law

Hawaii's Tax System

Hawaii's tax system is one of the most comprehensive among the fifty states. Virtually all potential sources of revenue, including gross receipts, income, inheritance, and real property, have been tapped. With the general prosperity of the islands in recent years, it has also proved to be highly productive.[1] It has provided sufficient revenue to permit a considerable expansion of current public services, while at the same time producing budgetary surpluses, some of which have been used for cash financing of capital improvements.[2]

From the administrative point of view, Hawaii has a highly centralized tax system. All major taxes are state administered and collected. There are no multiple local taxes, no personal property taxes, and no special levies for school districts. In fact, there are only two levels of local government in Hawaii, state and county.

While it is a major source of revenue for the counties, the real property tax is administered and collected by the state. The state government is responsible for the appraisal of all real property and establishes the annual net assessed valuation for each county. Each county government then determines its revenue needs and sets its tax rate accordingly. All revenue, except for reimbursement to the state for costs of assessment and collection, is turned over to the respective county government.

Although accounting for 80 percent of all county revenues today, the real property source has not traditionally been heavily utilized in Hawaii. As recently as eleven years ago, the territorial legislature imposed a flat dollar ceiling on the amount that could be collected from real property, thus depriving the counties of the benefits from increases in property values. Removal of this ceiling, the accelerated economic growth since Hawaii achieved statehood in 1959, and a concentrated effort by the tax authorities to update appraisals and assessments have combined to bring about a substantial increase in net assessed valuations.[3]

In addition to the increased valuations by the state, the county governments have increased their rates in an attempt to catch up on both current and capital requirements that had been forestalled by the previous unavailability of revenues. Even at this, real property tax collections have amounted to no more than 20 percent of total state revenues.[4] Tax rates, ranging from $15 per $1000 valuation for the rural county of Maui to more than $19 per $1000 for predominantly metropolitan Honolulu County, would seem moderate in comparison with the rates in other regions of the country.[5] These data, together with the expected continued increase in demand for public services, particularly those associated with urbanization, suggest that there will be an increasingly heavy reliance on the real property revenue source in Hawaii in the future.

The Hawaii tax system in recent years has also adopted a number of innovative features and procedures. For example, the 1965 State Legislature enacted a new series of tax credits to be applied against individual state income tax liability. Educational tax credits were allowed to provide assistance to taxpayers in meeting costs of education for dependents from kindergarten through higher educational levels. Provision was also made for a consumer tax credit to alleviate the relatively higher tax burden borne by low income persons under Hawaii's consumer-oriented general excise tax. Initial difficulties in administration of these new provisions have been experienced by the State Tax Department. It is too early to say whether the provisions are likely to accomplish their avowed objectives.

Hawaii's Land Use Law, though enacted in response to broader considerations, does afford a major opportunity for administrative innovation aimed at simplifying, systematizing, and equalizing assessment procedures and practices. Although the law is still unique to Hawaii, the conditions leading to its passage in 1961 and the problems with which it seeks to deal are not unlike those experienced in other parts of the nation. Thus, among the basic and, no doubt, familiar considerations leading to passage of the law were protection of productive agricultural lands from urban encroachment, prevention of scattered and premature development, restraint on land speculation, and preservation of unique natural assets. The conditions giving particular urgency to enactment of the law in Hawaii were the rapid economic growth experienced by the islands in recent years, the concentration of this growth in the Honolulu metropolitan area, and the growing scarcity of usable land to accommodate this growth.

The Land Use Law provides for state zoning authority to define boundaries of major land use and administer such land uses. Since one of the arguments advanced for its passage was the inadequacy of guidelines for land assessment according to best use, the law requires the State Department of Taxation, when making assessments, to consider the legally constituted land uses. Thus, it may be said that the continuing objectives of the Land Use Law are to preserve and encourage development of lands to their most suitable uses. Discussion of the Hawaiian experience may bring out insights which will contribute to improved property tax administration generally.

Conditions that Necessitated the Land Use Law

Population Growth

Hawaii has had an extremely rapid population growth over the past two decades; the resident population was estimated at 500,000 in 1950, 633,000 in 1960, and 746,000 in 1965.[6] In the decade from 1955 to 1965, Hawaii's resident population increased by 40 percent, more than twice the rate of growth in the nation as a whole (the nation's population increased by 18.4 percent in the same period). In the five years of 1960–65, the state's population increased by 8.1 percent.

The main sources of this population growth have been net in-migration of civilians other than military dependents and natural increase—births in excess of deaths.

Hawaii's crude birth rate has declined rather precipitously over the decade. Live births in the state declined from a rate of 34.7 per 1000 *de facto* civilian population in fiscal 1955 to 24.6 per 1000 population in fiscal 1965.

Civilian deaths, 6.3 per 1000 *de facto* civilian population in fiscal 1955, fell to an all-time low of 5.3 per 1000 civilian *de facto* population in 1965.

Notwithstanding the declining birth rate, the state's population continues to be very youthful as compared with mainland averages. In 1960, according to the United States Census, the median age of the nation's population was 29.5 years of age; that of the resident population of Hawaii was 24.3 years of age. Youthfulness of the state's population comes about in part from the relatively large number of military families in the population, military personnel and their dependents being younger on the average than the nation's nonmilitary families. But relative youthfulness is also a characteristic of the civilians who have moved into the state in the past few years, as it is of Hawaii's "native" population. In the census of 1960, the state's civilian population—excluding military dependents—then had a median age of 26 years.

Hawaii experienced a large net out-migration of population in the decade prior to 1955, when many of its families moved to the mainland, and elsewhere, in search of jobs. In contrast, the large influx of civilian population during the past decade has paralleled increased economic activity in the state. Very few of the civilian family heads who have moved to Hawaii in recent years have either been retired or had intentions of an immediate retirement. On the contrary, an overwhelming percentage of the newcomers have gone to the state to work.

Thus, the state's active work force has grown apace with its population, and the rate of unemployment in Hawaii has, for several years, been substantially lower than that in the nation as a whole.

It is not certain that the recent in-migrants have come to the state solely because of economic pressures or because economic opportunities seemed greater in Hawaii than in the areas from which they came; yet it is clear that increasing economic opportunities in Hawaii have at least made it possible for the newcomers to move to the state.

County Patterns

The lion's share of Hawaii's population is on the island of Oahu, which comprises (together with a few minor outlying islets) the city and the county of Honolulu. Estimates as of July 1, 1965, placed 82.3 percent of the state's resident population on Oahu. Honolulu is the single metropolitan area, and the center of transportation, commerce, tourism, and most of the state's nonagricultural industry.

It is on Oahu, moreover, that the population of the state has been growing most rapidly. During most of the period since World War II, the population of the neighbor islands has been undergoing a rather sharp decline. The reasons appear to be much the same as those for the decline of population in farm areas of the mainland. Economic activity on the neighbor islands has traditionally been almost wholly in agriculture, principally sugar cane and pineapple growing. But technological changes in agriculture in the years since World War II have resulted in rapid increases in output per hour of work and have sharply reduced the demand for agricultural labor. In consequence, families have moved from the neighbor islands to Oahu and the mainland in response to a growing demand for labor in these areas.

Qualified observers generally believe that the economies of the neighbor islands have now reached the "take-off" stage and that these islands will show new growth in the decade ahead. A number of resort hotels have recently been built on these islands, especially on Maui and Hawaii, and the state has undertaken a program of actively promoting tourist developments and tourist visits to the islands. Indeed, if the state's tourist industry continues to grow as expected, it will be almost a necessity that larger and larger numbers of visitors be accommodated on the neighbor islands. The state has also undertaken a large capital improvements program—road building, waterworks, and so on—for this purpose.

Employment

While defense activities, tourism, and tropical agriculture are Hawaii's three most important sources of income, no one of these industries directly accounts for as much income or employment as do aggregations of diverse other industry groups. The main sources of personal income in the state consist of those occupations by which the work force provides for its own needs, such as through retail, wholesale, service, and construction activities.

Several notable trends in the industrial composition of employment have been in evidence since World War II and perhaps earlier. The most noteworthy of these has been a relative decline in employment in agricultural pursuits because of automation, with a concomitant increase in urban, industrial employment of the work force. This shift has not been accompanied by a decline in agricultural output but in reduced labor requirements per unit of production.

In general, the trends following World War II continued in the 1960–65 period. Although agriculture had accounted for 23.1 percent of the employment in 1950, it accounted for only 6.5 percent in 1965. Building construction, which accounted for 7.5 percent of the employment in 1950, accounted for 10.2 percent in 1965, reflecting in part the state's recent construction boom. And as was the pattern on the mainland, relatively large numbers of workers shifted to the services sectors of the economy. Thus, 13.0 percent of the private employment was in services in 1950 and 22.2 percent in 1965.

Hawaii's tourist industry has recently shown the largest expansion of any of its major industries and is expected to be a principal factor for economic expansion in the state in the years immediately ahead. There were 606,000 visitors to the islands in 1965 as compared to 297,000 in 1960. Estimated expenditures of these visitors increased from $131,000,000 in 1960 to $265,000,000 last year.

Hawaii's sugar industry has shown a strong and continuing growth, with only moderate year-to-year production variations because of weather conditions. The crop marketed in 1966 had a value of $175,000,000, the highest in history except for that in 1963, a year of abnormally high prices for sugar. Marketings in 1965 were 38 percent above those of 1960. This industry is highly mechanized and is characterized by a very high output per worker, as compared with both beet sugar and sugar cane industries of other areas. Productivity has shown continuous and healthy gains, both in yields per acre of cane grown and in output per man hour of work.

Hawaii's pineapple industry, on the other hand, has expanded little in recent years, principally because of the introduction of pineapple growing into new producing areas of the world and rising competition from these areas in supplying markets on the United States mainland. Sales in 1965, at $119,000,000, were slightly below those of the previous year. This industry is expected to show only moderate growth in the years ahead, but nevertheless to remain one of the mainstays of the economy.

Economic Prospects

Basically, in recent years, the Hawaiian economy has proved adaptable to external changes, while developing increasing internal strength and stability at the same time. Although this past performance can reasonably be expected to continue into the future, it also can be seen that this economy may readily be disrupted by factors beyond its control. For example, the level of federal expenditures is dependent upon changes in the international situation and on national policy decisions which may be made to counteract or adjust to such changes. These factors can lead to a continuation or acceleration of recent trends or, on the other hand, to a wholesale disruption or dislocation of economic activity. Hawaii's tourist industry has benefited from prosperity conditions on the mainland and, indeed, throughout the world, from technological improvements in air transportation, and from increasing consumer preference for travel and recreation. Although continued favorable developments are anticipated, there is no guarantee of them. Political uncertainties, such as changes in Hawaii's share of the quota under the United States Sugar Act or revisions in tariffs on food products, can affect the well-being of some of its basic industries in the future.

Hawaii lacks local sources of energy usable by presently available technology, and it lacks a wide range of industrial materials available to other advanced economies. On the other hand, it has an abundance of human, climatic, and scenic resources and, prospectively, access to an abundance of untapped ocean resources. In addition, the state has locational advantages for international trade in a variety of products and services, as yet incompletely identified, and for processing industries geared to local consumption, to inter-regional trade, or both—also incompletely identified.

In view of this complex of limited but rather distinctive resources, it has become increasingly apparent that systematic identification and evaluation of the alternative uses of these resources is necessary, as is concerted effort to conserve them and realize their most productive uses.

Land Use

Present and potential uses of Hawaii's limited land supply are closely linked to ownership, basic suitabilities, and location.[7] These factors determine both the limits and the possibilities of land development.

Four basic land classes, designated as A, B, C, and D, have been set forth by the Land Study Bureau of the University of Hawaii. In general, lands in Class A are best suited for intensive agriculture. Those in Class B are moderately suited for intensive cultivation. Class C lands have only fair to marginal agricultural suitability. Lands in Class D are generally unsuited for intensive agriculture, but often are well suited for grazing, forestry, watershed, recreational, and urban uses.

A classification completed in 1961 indicated that, while the island of Oahu (city and county of Honolulu) comprises only 10 percent of the state's land area, it embraces 54 percent of the land best suited for intensive agriculture. In contrast, the island of Hawaii comprises almost two-thirds of the total land area, but has only one percent of the Class A land. However, this island has nearly half of the state's Class B land.[8]

On Oahu, 71 percent of the land is in private holdings. Of this, about 70 percent is in units of 5000 acres or more. Significantly, about two-thirds of Oahu's Class A land is in these large holdings. Approximately half of the Class B land is also in large private holdings. The lands least suited to intensive agriculture are primarily publicly owned or administered.[9]

Agriculture is the principal form of land use in Hawaii, encompassing approximately 87 percent of the total land area of the state. Of the land area in agricultural use, 60 percent is in grazing. Forest reserves occupy the next largest area, about 28 percent of the total agricultural land. The other major agricultural uses are sugar cane and pineapple production; these crops occupy about 11 percent of the lands in agricultural use. Diversified agriculture occupies about one percent.[10]

Of the land used in nonagricultural pursuits, about half is set aside for national parks or other public functions. Areas used for urban purposes and by military establishments are nearly equal, each comprising about 1.5 percent of the land area of the state.

The pattern of land use differs among the major islands of the state. For example, more land on Oahu is used for urban and military purposes than on any other island. The portion of Oahu devoted to plantation and diversified agriculture is also greater than that of any other island.

Hawaii's recent population and economic growth, concentrated in the city and county of Honolulu, have placed severe pressures on land use patterns. While Honolulu or the island of Oahu represents less than 10 percent of the total land area of the state, it has 80 percent of the population, with a density of more than 800 persons per square mile. As a consequence of this growth, urban development has pressed heavily into the countryside, and some of the better agricultural lands have passed into nonagricultural uses.[11] At the same time, demand for use of agricultural land, both to maintain the level of plantation crop exports and to expand the production of fresh foods for local consumption, has remained high.

A further consequence of this urban encroachment has been sharp increases in land values and taxes, resulting in decreasing efficiency of agricultural operations. Productive lands have therefore been withdrawn prematurely from income-yielding operations and have been forced into the market for urban development by natural economic law. Because of such pressures, landowners have been reluctant to renew the long-term leases under which many of the large agricultural operations are carried out. The lessees in turn have been discouraged from making the improvements or repairs needed to maintain agricultural efficiency.

These uncontrolled and uncoordinated responses to market pressures have resulted in scattered housing subdivisions or "urban sprawl," which has in turn increased the costs of providing community services and facilities.

These consequences of economic growth and urbanization stressed the need for comprehensive, long-range planning both to preserve and protect prime agricultural lands and to encourage the orderly development of urban areas to assure economy and efficiency in public services. However, planning without the statutory means of making it effective can be a meaningless academic exercise. The Hawaii Land Use Law represents a pioneering attempt to put "teeth" into the planning process.

Hawaii's Land Use Law

Hawaii's Land Use Law has evolved into a basic tool for the implementation of the state's general plan. The state plan represents, fundamentally, an expression of public policies and a process for relating public decisions to social, economic, and physical developments.

The state general plan was originally issued in 1961 in response to the following purported needs: (1) to foster economic growth and expanded opportunities, particularly on the neighbor islands; (2) to preserve the essential physical, economic, and social unity of the islands; and (3) to encourage the wise utilization of land. In its continuing refinement, the underlying concept has changed from the preparation of physical layouts indicating proposed land utilization patterns to a dynamic planning process that stresses policy formulation and decision-making on the basis of the best-informed judgment of the course of future events. However, the framers of the initial general plan did provide the groundwork for the more dynamic approach to comprehensive planning in calling for legislation to control the use of the land areas of the state.

The findings and "Declaration of Purpose" of the Land Use Law bear out its basic relationships with the general plan and express specific public concerns, policies, and objectives:

> Inadequate controls have caused many of Hawaii's limited and valuable lands to be used for purposes that may have a short-term gain to a few but result in a long-term loss to the income and growth potential of our economy. Inadequate bases for assessing lands according to their value in those uses that can best serve both the well-being of the owner and the well-being of the public have resulted in inequities in the tax burden, contributing to the forcing of land resources into uses that do not best serve the welfare of the State. Scattered subdivisions with expensive, yet reduced, public services; the shifting of prime agricultural lands into nonrevenue producing residential uses when other lands are available that could serve adequately the urban needs; failure to utilize fully multiple-purpose lands; these are evidences of the need for public concern and action.
>
> Therefore, the Legislature finds that in order to preserve, protect and encourage the development of the lands in the State for those uses to which they are best suited for the public welfare and to create a complementary assessment basis according to the contribution of the lands in those uses to which they are best suited, the power to zone should be exercised by the State and the methods of real property assessment should encourage rather than penalize those who would develop these uses.[12]

The act provided for the establishment of a State Land Use Commission, consisting of nine members. Seven of these are appointed by the governor, one member from each of six senatorial districts and one at-large member. The director of the Department of Planning and Economic Development and the chairman of the Board of Land and Natural Resources serve on the commission as *ex officio* voting members.

In its original form, the act called for classification of all land in the state into three districts: urban, agricultural, and conservation. Subsequent legislation added a fourth district, rural, primarily at the behest of the neighbor island legislators, who foresaw a transitional situation with an intermixing of urban and agricultural pursuits.

The act leaves intact the zoning powers previously granted to the counties, with the exception that restrictions are placed on urban zoning for any land outside an urban district established by the State Land Use Commission. Zoning power within conservation districts is retained by the State Department of Land and Natural Resources. The act details specific procedures and time limits within which the commission has established, first, temporary district boundaries and, later, permanent boundaries.

Procedures are provided for public hearings on rules and regulations adopted by the commission, as well as for petitions by landowners and state and local governmental agencies requesting boundary amendments and variances. The act requires that the commission make a comprehensive review of its land classifications and land use regulations every five years. Included in the act are provisions under which the Department of Taxation must consider the land use districts in the establishment of tax assessments. In this connection, the law provides that owners may dedicate land to a specific use within an agricultural district for a minimum period of ten years, during which time the land will be assessed at its value in such use.

Land Use Districts

Urban.—The basic identification of urban districts is given in the act as "areas characterized by city-like concentrations by people, structures, streets and other related land uses." The act requires a complete resurvey of all district boundaries at intervals of five years.[13] A period of ten years has been adopted as the practicable and adequate planning period for estimating the requirements of urban growth. As provided by state law, county planning authorities had jurisdiction for planning and zoning in their respective counties, and Act 187 recognizes this jurisdiction in the urban districts.

The estimated area for urban expansion has been allocated primarily according to probable and desirable growth in view of potential economic development, available public facilities, and employment opportunities. These several considerations have led to a liberal allocation of land in some urban areas whereas other communities are expected to realize their full appropriate growth within their present limits.

An important factor in the allocation of land for urban expansion is the requirement by the act to preserve prime agricultural land. Such land has been recommended for inclusion within urban districts only in areas where adequate land in appropriate locations within the county is not available for the estimated urban expansion during the next ten years.

In the allocation of land for urban development, the attempt was made to avoid further scatteration of urban facilities and the accompanying burden of extension of public utilities. Some areas in which dwellings are sparsely located have been excluded from urban districts.

Agricultural.—The act defines agriculture as "the raising of livestock or the growing of crops, flowers, foliage, or other products," and requires that the greatest possible protection be given to those lands with a high capacity for intensive cultivation. The allocation of land for agricultural districts was based upon an analysis of the soil classification, existing land uses for agriculture, topography and rainfall, and state-owned land currently leased for agricultural purposes.

Planning and zoning jurisdiction in the agricultural district is vested in the county authorities, subject to the regulations adopted by the Land Use Commission.

Conservation.—Act 187 establishes a conservation district for the purpose of "protecting watersheds and water supplies; preserving scenic areas; providing parkland, wilderness and beach reserves; conserving endemic plants, fish, and wildlife; preventing floods and soil erosion; forestry; and other related activities." These requirements of the act have been examined and followed in the recommended conservation districts. In evaluation of the requirements, a principal criterion has been the presence of an overriding state-wide concern for the public interest.

Rural.—The subsequent amendment to the Land Use Law, which provided for the addition of a fourth district, defined that district to include "activities or uses as characterized by low density residential lots of not more than one dwelling house per one-half acre in areas where 'city-like' concentration of people, structures, streets and urban level of services are absent, and where small farms are intermixed with such low density residential lots. These districts may include contiguous areas which are not suited to low density residential lots or small farms by reason of topography, soils, and other related characteristics."[14]

While there is already evidence of the effectiveness of the Land Use Law, its real value to the public welfare will become much more obvious in the long run. Thus far, actual experience with the administration of the law shows that urban developments on prime agricultural lands and scattered developments have been discouraged, and conservation interests have been substantially expanded.

The various attempts to repeal the law or soften its provisions may be offered as further testimony to its effectiveness to date.

Conclusions

The Hawaiian Land Use Law has not been operative long enough to permit any meaningful conclusions with respect to its influence on real property assessment practices or results in the state. Such observations should probably await at least the fuller achievement of the direct objectives of the law—namely, the legal protection or preservation of land for stipulated purposes and provision of an orderly mechanism integrated with a comprehensive planning process to assure the proper development and utilization of the state's basic land resources.

Nevertheless, the potential for greater consistency and uniformity in assessment practices, which follows from effective administration of the Land Use Law, can be recognized. The law requires that the land use districts be taken as a basis for property assessment so as to encourage rather than penalize those who make the best use of their lands. In this sense, an additional legal check point is provided for the assessor in determining his land use classifications. In the state of Hawaii, the assessor is required also to consider zoning established by the counties. In case of overlap or contradiction among agencies, zoning by the counties is given preference, although the question might be raised as to why the higher level of jurisdiction should not supersede.

However, it should be noted that the land use classification by the assessor cannot exceed the zoning by the county or State Land Use Commission; it may be less than that permitted by established zoning. Zoning sets the upper limits of classification and may consequently serve to check unreasonable or unanticipated upward valuations in the process.

The urban districts established under the Land Use Law provide for population growth and related urban requirements over a ten-year period. Given the proper designation of such areas, the tax assessor can proceed with his day-to-day determinations, supported and checked by legally established long-term guidelines. Under these circumstances, property tax administration could well become a positive influence for the stimulation of economic growth on an orderly basis, rather than a passive, or even negating, influence on the welfare and progress of a community.

Notes

1 Tax collections increased by 50 percent from $175,000,000 in fiscal 1963 to $262,000,000 in fiscal 1966 (State of Hawaii, Department of Taxation, *Annual Reports* for years shown).

2 Per capita direct expenditures by state and local governments in Hawaii increased from $372 in 1960 to $494 in 1965, and Hawaii ranked fifth among all states in 1965 in this category (United States Department of Commerce, *Governmental Finances*).

3 Net assessed valuations increased from $2,300,000,000 in 1963 to $3,000,000,000 in 1966 (State of Hawaii, Department of Taxation, *Annual Reports*).

4 *Ibid.* Property tax revenue is estimated by the author to be 2.4 percent of the gross state product in Hawaii in 1966 as compared with 3.4 percent of the gross national product for the country as a whole in 1963, as cited in Dick Netzer, *Economics of the Property Tax* (Washington, 1966).

5 Netzer cites effective tax rates (property tax revenues divided by estimated market values) as 0.7 percent for Hawaii, compared with a national average of 1.4 percent in 1960.

6 Statistical data and analysis in this section are from various publications of the Department of Planning and Economic Development, State of Hawaii. See, particularly, *The State of Hawaii Data Book* (1967) and *The Hawaiian Economy: Problems and Prospects* (1966).

7 The discussion in this section draws upon various State of Hawaii publications. See, particularly, H. L. Baker, *The Land Situation in the State of Hawaii* (1961); Hawaii State Planning Office, *The Protection and Zoning of Rural, Agricultural, and Urban Lands* (1961).

8 Baker, *Land Situation,* p. 8.

9 *Ibid.*

10 *Ibid.,* p. 9.

11 It should be recalled that more than half of the state's prime agricultural lands are located on Oahu.

12 *Act 187, Session Laws of Hawaii* (1961).

13 The discussion of land use districts draws heavily upon the officially adopted *State Land Use District Regulations* (June 20, 1964) and the report, *Land Use Districts for the State of Hawaii,* prepared by Harland Bartholomew and Associates (1963).

14 *Act 205, Session Laws of Hawaii* (1963).

12 Ronald B. Welch

Property Taxation:
Policy Potentials and Probabilities

If California is typical of the nation, the property tax is the most unpopular of all major taxes now employed in the United States. It is under attack from all sides. It is denounced by welfare economists as our most regressive major tax, by businessmen as our most inflexible major tax, by farmers as our most unfair tax, by the aged as our tax least related to ability to pay, by guardians of the law as our most dishonestly assessed tax, by students of government as our most ineptly administered tax, and by conscious or instinctive disciples of Henry George as our most repressive tax. Indeed, it is hard to find anyone who will say a good word for the property tax as we know it in this country.

Why, then, does it continue to flourish—to bring hundreds of millions more each year into local government treasuries? Mainly because, by tradition, it is in large part a locally administered tax and one whose rates are generally set by locally elected legislative bodies. The tradition of local administration is often bolstered with the assertion that the property tax is well suited to local administration, and this assertion is infrequently challenged.[1] Local establishment of tax rates is more often challenged—by means of constitutional or statutory rate limitations that are restrictive enough to deprive local governments of meaningful rate-setting powers.

Despite its severe critics and its limited virtues, no one now predicts the early demise or even significant atrophy of the property tax. This is not to say that there will be no shrinkage in the scope of the tax but rather that reductions in scope will probably be fully or largely offset by growth of the economy and rate increases. The amazingly rapid spread of inventory exemption in the last few years seems to be gaining momentum, and this exemption may touch off a new round of homestead exemptions. Exemption of institutional and private housing occupied by elderly persons is adding many millions of dollars to the exemption figures. Farmers are gaining what amounts to partial exemption in many states on the improbable claim that tax reduction will preserve open spaces. Those who seek total personal property exemption—an administrative incubus—have probably not made their last converts. Indeed, the only organized exemption movement which seems to have made little progress on the mainland is the one popularly known as the single tax movement.

There is one bright spot in this rather discouraging outlook. We can expect improvements in property tax administration to continue at the rather rapid pace that has been set during the last thirty years. Although good property tax administration made its debut in the United States around 1900, it spread to only a few large cities during the first third of the century. The second third of the twentieth century saw its widespread dissemination. What does the last third of the century hold in store?

I see two promising developments. The first of these is a much wider use by assessment review agencies of the average assessment-level findings of state tax departments. The second is a much wider and more sophisticated use of sales data by assessing agencies.

Use of Assessment-Level Findings by Assessment Review Agencies

It has long been observed that a poorly equalized assessment roll is improved little or not at all by the hierarchy of agencies that has been established to second-guess the assessor. The failure of assessment review agencies has been attributable to many things, but not the least of them is the common requirement that an appellant taxpayer demonstrate that his property is excessively assessed in comparison with properties similar in type and location. While such a comparison may afford some protection against the most blatant forms of fraud or incompetence, it is incapable of remedying the garden variety of inequality which flourishes in almost every assessment district—inequality between properties of different types and in different areas.

Theoretically, a property owner is entitled to an assessment that bears the same relation to the property's value as the assessment of all other property in the taxing district bears to the value of such other property.[2] When more than one district is levying taxes on the property and the districts are not coterminous, this ideal equality is obtainable only when the average assessment ratio for each of the taxing districts is equal. The ideal is likely to be a far cry from reality. The next best approximation of equality is obtained when a person's property is assessed at a proportion of its value that equals the average assessment ratio for the district that levies the highest of the rates to which the property in question is subject—a district that may or may not be responsible for the performance of the assessment function. As a practical matter, however, about the best that can be expected of an assessment review agency is that it will equalize the assessment ratio of an appellant's property with the average assessment ratio for the taxing district that conducts the original assessment function—the county in the western and southern states and a smaller unit of government in most of the eastern and midwestern states.

It is only within the last few years that reasonably reliable average assessment ratios have been available for all assessment districts in many states. But the use of these ratios by assessment review agencies is even more recent.[3] In California we have published assessment ratios for counties since 1960, and not until 1967 were the ratios being used by our county equalization agencies. Their use has not been of the review agencies' own volition but by reason of a wide-ranging assessment reform bill that was enacted in 1966 after an assessment scandal had rocked the state.

The necessity for using our ratios in California is well illustrated in exaggerated form by the situation in San Francisco. Here the assessor who was removed from office after being convicted of bribery and conspiracy in 1966 purported to assess property at 50 percent of its full cash value. Our ratio findings for the area since 1960 had been in the neighborhood of 20 to 24 percent. But when a property owner appealed an assessment, he was expected to demonstrate that his assessment was more than 50 percent of his property's value. Needless to say, with an average assessment level of less than 25 percent, few applicants could do this and few even tried. When I asked an intelligent member of the county equalization agency why he gave no credence to our ratios for the county, he appeared to be ignorant of our ratios and to have been naively credulous of the assessor's assertions. His excuse was that he had no other source than the assessor for information on the ratio for particular types of property.

It is interesting to note that the two California county assessors who have been convicted of crimes and the one who took his own life in connection with the recent assessment scandals purported to use a much higher ratio of assessed to full value than they actually used. Conversely, no assessor who purported to be assessing at a ratio that exceeded our ratio finding by less than 50 percent has been convicted by the courts or by his own hand. A purported ratio that vastly exceeds the average ratio is a perfect setting for fraud and the kinds of immorality that are inevitably associated with fraud.

The obvious solution is to require the assessment review agency to take cognizance of an assessment district's actual assessment level as established by an impartial state agency. But there are two reasons why this solution is likely to result in unwarranted reductions in assessments: the tendency for assessors to be deliberately conservative in their appraisals and the tendency for average assessment levels to fall below the assessor's objective because of rising price levels and the assessor's inability to reappraise all properties each year.

Consider, first, a situation in which property values are stagnant and the assessor purports to assess at full value but appraises property conservatively, with the result that the state tax department finds an average assessment ratio of 80 percent. When an appellant goes before an assessment review agency, equity will seldom be dispensed by applying the state's 80 percent ratio to the *assessor's* appraised value. The assessment review agency must start with a higher appraised value than the assessor's if it is to use the state's ratio. There are, to my knowledge, only three means by which it can obtain the higher appraised value: (1) by making its own appraisal—if need be with its own staff—rather than merely hearing the assessor, the appellant, and witnesses called by the appellant; (2) by permitting the assessor to bring in new evidence of value that, in effect, indicts the value he placed on the roll; and (3) by establishing a rebuttable presumption that the assessor's appraised value is too low in the proportion that the state's ratio falls below the ratio which the assessor applied to his conservative appraised values.

The first of these means is used in Oregon, where the county board of equalization is required to employ an appraiser, but it is not common practice. Usually, the administrative review agency is like a court; it listens to the evidence presented by the appellant and the assessor and is required to reach a decision on the property's value that is supported by the evidence. Since the assessee is not likely to testify to a value higher than the one on which the assessment was predicated, the assessor's appraised value will normally be the highest value in evidence. Unless the assessor is permitted—and encouraged—to bring in a new appraised value higher than the one on which he based the original assessment, equalization at the state-found ratio means that the appellant will receive an unwarranted reduction in assessed value. Chances are, however, that the assessor will not often indict his assessed value even though permitted or encouraged to do so.

The third means of avoiding unwarranted reductions by assessment review agencies—by establishing a rebuttable presumption that the true value of the property whose assessment is appealed exceeds the assessor's appraised value in the proportion that the assessor's purported ratio exceeds the state's ratio finding—is the only workable solution to the problem in most states. In the above illustration, the state having found a ratio of 80 percent, the true value of each property whose assessment is appealed would be rebuttably presumed to be 125 percent (i.e., 100 ÷ 80) of the assessor's appraised value. Anyone whose property was appraised by the assessor at more than 80 percent of true value would then have the opportunity to rebut the presumption that his property was worth 125 percent of the assessor's appraised value. Those whose property was appraised by the assessor at 80 percent of true value or less would not be able, merely by standing on the assessor's appraised value, to make a case for relief—to which they obviously are not entitled.

If every property were assessed at 80 percent of true value, the main objections to giving all appellants relief are that not every property owner would appeal and that the appellate process would be an expensive nuisance if all *did* appeal. But the fact is that an average ratio of 80 percent undoubtedly is accompanied by considerable dispersion about the average. Some properties will be assessed as high as 100 percent; others at 50 or 60 percent. *Those whose properties are assessed at more than 80 percent will be benefited by a rebuttable presumption that their properties are worth 25 percent more than the assessor's appraised value.* It is not surprising, however, that taxpayers do not understand this and that in California we have been unable to obtain legislative acceptance of the plan.

Mention was made above of a second reason why some individual assessments may be at a higher percentage of true value than the state's ratio finding for the assessment district. When land values and the general price level are rising and the assessor is unable to reappraise the whole district each year, the average assessment level will be less than 100 percent even though the assessor's appraisals were at full value when made. In California we think that 90 percent is about as high an average ratio as can be attained with the conventional assessment practices even though the assessor's appraisals are at full value as of the time they were made. To use the state's average ratio of 90 percent as the level to which the review agency equalizes assessments would frustrate the assessor's laudable efforts to appraise and assess at full value.

The solution to this second problem is to allow a reasonable tolerance above the state's average ratio finding within which an appealed assessment will not be lowered. The Advisory Commission on Intergovernmental Relations has recommended a 10 percent tolerance;[4] the California Legislature has enacted a 15 percent tolerance.[5] Without the rebuttable presumption to which I have previously referred, 15 percent is likely to prove too small; with the rebuttable presumption it might prove to be quite generous.

Use of Sales Data by Assessing Agencies

This second problem of assessments keeping pace with prices can be mitigated by effective use of sales data by assessors. Until recently, most assessors in California were following what we refer to as cyclical reappraisal policy—one in which the assessor concentrates his appraisal efforts in one part of the county one year and another part the next, covers the whole county in a period of three to six or more years, and then repeats the cycle. About six years ago we ceased to advise assessors to reappraise cyclically and urged that they concentrate their appraisal efforts in areas where analyses of ratios of assessed values to sales prices of individual properties produced large coefficients of dispersion or average ratios that varied widely from the countywide average.[6] By following this practice, an assessor can do a reasonably good job of keeping his countywide average up even though he is able to reappraise only a small fraction of the county each year.

More recently we have developed another technique that we think is highly promising. This technique provides for production of tentative appraised values by computer, using multiple regression analysis. Thus far we have applied the technique only to single-family residences, but we believe it can be used in the appraisal of multiple-family residences and possibly some other property types.

When the technique is applied to single-family residences, recent sales prices constitute the dependent variable. The independent variables are the many measurable facts that buyers and sellers are assumed to take into account when negotiating a sale. The number of independent variables that can be employed is legion. In San Francisco, because a crash program was instituted by the new assessor who took office in 1966, we used only eight independent variables which happened, almost by chance, to be recorded on computer tapes. In Orange County we are using over 100 variables which will be accumulated for the county's 300,000 single-family residences over the next year or two.[7]

The most desirable independent variables are those which are precisely measurable and either which do not change over a property's lifetime or of whose change the assessor is automatically notified in the event of a change. Lot dimensions, building dimensions where building permits are required, and zoning are illustrative of these variables. Variables which change without automatic notification of the assessor but which can be measured by the assessor without returning to the property, such as replacement cost, are almost as desirable. Least desirable, other things being equal, are variables which are very difficult to measure accurately, such as view and other locational amenities, those variables which change frequently, and those whose change can be observed and measured only by field inspection of individual properties.

Locational amenities are important determinants of residential land values and cannot be ignored even though they are difficult to measure and require occasional field review. Their use can be minimized, however, by the development of different regression equations for different areas. If locational amenities were exactly equal within an area, there would be no such variables in the equation. But to confine the equations to such

small areas would so severely limit the dependent variable observations (sales prices) that it would be necessary to accumulate sales data over an excessively long period of time.[8] Therefore, even if for no other reason, it is desirable to derive equations that are applicable to fairly large, yet fairly homogeneous
areas and to use some measures of locational amenities. In our
Orange County experimental work, for example, we have used
view and neighborhood value trends even though their measurement is highly subjective.

At the risk of going into excessive detail, I will describe the
regression analysis thoroughly before speaking of the results
of the tests to which we have subjected it.

The first step was to define each area within which a separate regression equation was to be developed. In Orange
County we selected five areas; in San Francisco, eighteen areas.
Sales prices of single-family residences in each area were then
assembled. In Orange County we used sales during the past
one or two years; in San Francisco, those during a two- or
three-year period. At this point, we could have purified the
sales data by culling out sales with characteristics that are
widely considered to make them poor evidence of value and
perhaps by adjusting some sales prices to what we refer to as
cash equivalents;[9] we did only a limited amount of purification
for what we deemed to be good reasons. The next step was to
list many variables that, in the opinion of professional appraisers, are important determinants of sales prices. These variables
for each of the sold properties were then measured and recorded.

Now we were ready to compute a regression equation. The
dependent and independent variables were fed into the computer, which identified first the most highly correlated independent variable, then the independent variable most highly
correlated with the remaining unexplained variations in selling price, and so on, until all variables which contributed significantly $(f = 1.00)$ to the explanation of variations in sales
prices were identified. The computer then produced a multiple regression equation in which weights were assigned to each
of the independent variables. This equation could be used,

within the area for which it was developed, to compute the expected selling price of any single-family residence for which the independent variables were known.

The next step was to test the equation by applying it to the properties whose sales had been used to develop the equation. This test produced *probable* selling prices that were then compared with *actual* selling prices. Ratios of probable selling prices to actual selling prices were computed, together with coefficients of dispersion of the ratios. These coefficients in the five areas tested in Orange County ranged from 2.3 percent to 4.8 percent. In other words, had the equations been used to appraise the properties that were sold, half the appraised values would have been within 2.3 percent of the actual selling prices in the best area and within 4.8 percent in the poorest. Thus the poorest of these coefficients is less than half the best dispersion coefficient that the nation's most accurate assessors have been able to achieve.[10]

The acid test will come, of course, as the equation is applied to unsold homes and the estimated selling prices are compared with subsequent sales prices. In Orange County, the test must await the acquisition, coding, and storage of data on the variables for the unsold properties. The San Francisco values were used in the preparation of an assessment roll that was completed about July 1, 1967. Between that date and February 28, 1968, there were 1418 sales of single-family residences whose assessed values were based on computer-produced full values. The coefficient of dispersion of the ratios of assessed value to sales price (the average deviation from the median divided by the median) was 12.4 percent. This is approximately equal to the lowest coefficients of dispersion for single-family dwellings in California counties using conventional appraisal techniques[11] and far below the coefficient of 17.1 percent for those San Francisco single-family residences that had been assessed in 1968 on the basis of ordinary field appraisals. Considering the crudeness and limited number of the independent variables that were available (number of stories, number of bathrooms, number of rooms, attached or detached, basement or no basement, zoning, year of construction, and square footage of living area), we felt that the program had passed the test with flying colors.

Most of the data to be collected in Orange County are the kind traditionally recorded by assessors, so this step is not a very costly process. When it has been accomplished, the prices of properties recently sold will be used, together with the independent variables for the same properties, to produce a new regression equation for each of the areas into which the county has been divided. Expected selling prices will then be computed for all single-family residences and will be supplied to the appraisal staff for a cursory field review to see whether any of the expected prices are obviously unacceptable. This process will be repeated each year, with newly acquired sales data, updated independent variables, and newly derived equations.

We anticipate that the end results of the program will be (1) assessed values of single-family residences that are kept abreast of market values by means of small annual changes instead of large changes at four- or five-year intervals; (2) better equalization of countywide taxes by the change of all single-family residence assessments each year instead of the change of assessments in one area one year, another the next; (3) better assessment of other properties because appraisal personnel are free to work on these properties; (4) lower overall expenditures on property tax assessment.

The advent of third-generation computers has made it economically feasible to apply multiple regression analysis to many problems that were not previously adaptable to this technique. We look forward to an exciting future for the computer in assessors' offices as it graduates from an accounting tool and a substitute for the desk calculator to a novel and valuable appraisal tool.

Notes

1 See, however, Advisory Commission on Intergovernmental Relations, *The Role of the States in Strengthening the Property Tax* (1963), I, 92–96.

2 I developed this point more fully in an unpublished paper

presented at the 25th Annual Conference of the National Association of Tax Administrators, 1957, Poland Spring, Maine. For a somewhat different viewpoint, see Francis J. Carr, "Measures of Central Tendency in Assessment Ratio Studies," *Revenue Administration—1959* (Proceedings of the 27th Annual Conference of the National Association of Tax Administrators, 1959), pp. 50–56.

3 Advisory Commission on Intergovernmental Relations, *Role of the States,* I, 145.

4 Advisory Commission on Intergovernmental Relations, *1965 State Legislative Program* . . . (October, 1964), pp. 40–41.

5 *Revenue and Taxation Code,* Sec. 1605, as amended by Ch. 147, Statutes of 1966 (1st Extraordinary Session).

6 Ronald B. Welch, "Maintaining Assessments," presented at the Annual Conference of the Western States Association of Tax Administrators, October 4, 1961; reprinted in *Assessors' News Letter* (International Association of Assessing Officers), December, 1961, pp. 147–150; January, 1962, p. 1.

7 Robert H. Gustafson, "E.S.P. and the Appraiser," in *Revenue Administration—1967* (Proceedings of the 35th Annual Conference of the National Association of Tax Administrators, 1967), pp. 62–67. Mr. Gustafson, Statistical Consultant in the California State Board of Equalization, working with assessors Joseph E. Tinney of San Francisco and Andrew J. Hinshaw of Orange County and their staffs, has developed the technique described in this section of my chapter.

8 This defect can be partially overcome by the use of elapsed time between a sale and the assessment date as one of the variables. Implicit in this usage, however, is the assumption that the relationship between price and date of sale is linear.

9 Ronald B. Welch, "Some Observations on Assessment Ratio Measurement," *National Tax Journal,* XVII (March, 1964), 19.

10 United States Bureau of the Census, *1962 Census of Governments, Taxable Property Values,* II, 140–53.

11 *Ibid.,* p. 141; see also the forthcoming volume in the *1967 Census of Governments.*

Conference Discussion

After the twelve papers in this volume were presented, the final session of the conference was devoted to a general discussion, over which Paul E. Alyea presided. An edited transcript of the discussion follows.

Paul E. Alyea: In my view, discussion in this concluding session well might take the form of an attempt to appraise the extent to which the conference has achieved its major objective, namely, "To consider whether and to what extent administrative problems, including the assessment process, are obstacles to land value taxation." Suppose that the legislature of one of our states should decide to confine the property tax base to land, with rates designed to recapture most economic rent? Could this be done, given the existing institutional context, administrative organization, appraisal techniques, and know-how of property taxation? Is land value taxation administrable? ,

The papers read at this conference covered a wide range of topics relating to property taxation. The problems covered are not new. They range from broad equity issues of perennial concern to essentially technical matters of valuation and administrative organization. What inferences which bear on the conference objective may be drawn from the papers?

One of the more optimistic conclusions is that property tax administration has been improving at an accelerated rate, as local review agencies make more use of centrally determined average assessment ratios and as assessing agencies make better use of sales data. Assessment of land separate from improvements remains a problem. Perhaps some of you will respond to the question whether this can be successfully accomplished.

Another issue, made explicit in some papers and implicit in others, bears directly on the policy of valuation in terms of highest and best use, particularly in urban-fringe areas. Wherein lies the public interest? Who is to determine it? How is it to be determined? Can we achieve such ends as preservation of adequate open space, control of urban sprawl, and equitable treatment of present owners, by following a tough-minded policy of taxing on the basis of market values when these are in excess of the capitalized income from *present* highest and best use? Do we need to employ some device for granting preferential treatment to existing owners with some provision for subsequent recapture of socially generated gains? If so, can this be accomplished without resort to some variation of self-assessment, with appropriate sanctions against underassessment, in those cases where realization of gains is unduly postponed?

Whatever conclusions we reach here will be both of general interest and of direct significance to future TRED planning.

It has been my feeling over the years that those interested in land value taxation must come to grips with the question of whether the tax can be administered. They must spell out the needed administrative pattern. While this conference has not voiced the last word on this matter, it has made at least a modest beginning.

Let us examine further to what extent administrative problems, including the assessment process, are obstacles to land value taxation.

Shelley Mark: I would say simply that, while there are administrative obstacles, I think that they are not irresolvable. Possibly with more experience with our [Hawaii's] Land Use Law and with closer coordination between the tax assessors in our state and those people who are responsible for the administration of the land use law, we will develop new points that will be pertinent to the resolution of this question in the future.

Kenneth C. Back: I feel that administration as such is not a bar in the way of land taxation. To my way of thinking, administration would be simpler under a system where you tax only the land than under a system taxing both land and buildings. I think it can be done, technically. It's a question of whether you want to do it, and I certainly have no position to take on that.

Alyea: Do you think we know how to do it now if we wanted to?

Back: I think so. I think technically it can be done. It is easier than when you value both land and improvements, because most of the problems in the assessor's office come in valuing buildings, in determining depreciation and obsolescence, and in trying to add on every bathroom. I would suppose, as a wild guess, that in most assessing offices probably five times as much time is spent on buildings as on land. I am speaking now of city assessment districts. I really don't know how that would work out in a rural county. One of the things that we are trying is to devote less time to buildings and more to land. We are simply not going to worry about all the refinements of doubtful value. We will devote more time to land valuation than to over-refinement of improvement values.

Property Taxation, Urban Expansion, Transitional Land Use, and Compensation Concepts

Peter House: Let me try to answer a question that has a great deal of significance for people interested in the land value tax.

Why should a farmer who is going to make a large capital

gain on his land feel imposed upon or unhappy about it? I think probably this question is important if you are going to levy a tax or change a tax system in order to move people off the land so that the land can go to a higher use.

I have done a lot of interviewing of farmers in Maryland and upstate New York asking questions about this point. I can give quickly several examples. One farmer had just sold his land. He had made three-quarters of a million dollars on the sale, which is an incredible capital gain. I sat with him on his porch. He had just come in from the field, apparently happy about the sale, and said, "I'm going to Florida." After I inquired, "What are you going to do in Florida?" he replied, "I don't know. I'll go down to Florida and go on a vacation." I asked, "Then what are you going to do?" and the sad answer came, "Well, I don't know. I suppose I'll—I really haven't thought about it." He sat for a few minutes and looked at his land. Finally he said, "Son, let me tell you something I haven't told anybody. I made a mistake. I'm too old to start again. I want to live back in Maryland, but I can't buy another farm because I don't want to start over." That's my first point.

My second example involves an upstate New York farmer who sold out for a highway interchange, because of his age. He took me out in back and said, "See those fields back there? See these rocks? Under that land it's tiled, and I did all of it. That fence over there, those rocks, I picked up every one of them and put them over there. I'm too old to do that again. That's my life, you know, laying out there."

A third, to give you another example of why money can't replace this sort of intangible, was a man who had quit farming and then had come back. He's rented his farm and come back. He said he just couldn't do without it. He was the sixth generation of farmers on that place. There are some things that can't be compensated for in money.

Property Tax Deferrals

William Vickrey: I think realistically, whether you can compensate the intangible loss adequately or not, you want to minimize the amount of it that takes place, and certainly the case of the fellow who's going to get three-quarters of a million dollars for his property in a voluntary sale is not like the second case where the place is being condemned for an interchange.

House: It wasn't condemned. He just happened to have a piece of land at an interchange and sold it, as it turned out, for an industrial site.

Vickrey: In that case, the industry could have gone elsewhere. If the land is ripe for development, despite the attachment of the individual to his land, the public interest is in turning over the land to the higher use, whatever price you may put on the tiles and the lot.

There are other cases where you have the marginal farmer who is really just making ends meet in terms of his day-to-day intake and outgo, with a mortgage on his farm. The farm is worth a great deal more than the mortgage now, but if you raise the assessment on him and don't provide any kind of provision for deferred payment of property taxes, he just won't have the cash to pay. Either he's going to have to sell out and move and go elsewhere with all of the destruction in individual values that this may entail, or, conceivably, he can get a new or adjusted mortgage. This would be fine if the mortgage market were that good. But you take the fellow who, several years ago, was fortunate enough to get a mortgage at 4 or 4½ percent, and it has quite a distance yet to run. If he wants to get some more money with which to pay the taxes, either he must turn over and pay off that mortgage and take out a new mortgage at 5½ to 6 percent, or he must take a second mortgage at 7 or 8 percent. Neither of these alternatives is particularly attractive, and it will be not only unfair but to some extent wasteful to compel this kind of financing rather than to go into tax deferral. Under these circumstances, I would put in a very strong plug for a tax deferral scheme.

Back: Why would you defer this particular individual and not others?

Vickrey: I'd defer a person who you can legitimately feel has an unrealized capital gain, one that is not necessarily appropriate to realize yet—that is, the land is ripening but not ripe.

Back: You would defer all underimprovements for the land? Anyone who didn't put the land to its highest and best use would get deferred?

Vickrey: No. Anyone for whom the value of the land is enhanced because of an approaching change in the appropriate use. The land is still in its highest and best use now, but the value of the land has suffered in appreciation, and the current use is not capable of earning a full cash return on the present value of the anticipated future development. That's the sort of thing I have in mind.

Mason Gaffney: I was reading recently a book by a professor at Columbia University, entitled *Agenda for Progressive Taxation,* in which it is alleged that unrealized capital gains should be taxed at the time that they accrue without waiting for realization. Is this consistent with the position you are now taking?

Vickrey: Yes, it's consistent. If you read a little bit farther in that volume, you will find that I admitted that this idea was not a practical proposition. At the time I wrote, it was because of administrative complexities, but there is a strong liquidity argument in general. The practical solution, even in the case of the income tax, is for the tax on the capital gain to be deferred until realization. But the deferral of the tax should be accompanied by an appropriate interest charge, so that, in effect, no advantage is realized in the long run by the deferment of the tax. You defer the tax, but you have to accumulate interest on what you have deferred.

Gaffney: Is that your present position, then?

Vickrey: The same. If you defer the amount of tax that's represented by the increased assessment, where the increased assessment is based not on current earning power but on the approach of a future better use, then whatever is deferred should bear interest. The taxpayer should have to pay interest at the time of the eventual sale or conversion.

Gaffney: This is the "Stocker proposal."

Vickrey: I think in the case I mentioned, it is, in a sense, inefficient to compel a person who is in a bad liquidity bind to have expensive methods of financing if you can avoid it. I would not regard this tax deferral as an abatement of the tax, but merely as an accommodation of the timing of payment.

House: Would this help to work out some of the imperfections of the market; in other words, to wait until the land really was ready?

Vickrey: It would avoid a good many forced sales, I imagine.

Alyea: You are saying it's a little better to have a farm continuing in operation than for the site to become an automobile graveyard.

Vickrey: Yes, or to have a speculator buy it and leave it fallow. I think more important than the agricultural production from the farm is, in many cases, simply the human satisfaction that the farmer gets from staying there.

Frederick Stocker: I'd endorse that. I think the case for the tax deferral in areas where you have no land use planning or controls essentially boils down to an equity argument, and to justify it on the ground that it's going to produce some better pattern of land use is mighty tenuous.

Gaffney: Mr. Back asked, it seems to me, an important question. If you are going to do this for this particular class of taxpayers, why not for others?

Where you have cases of individuals wallowing in self-pity over circumstances of life which afflict other people, many of them without the compensation of the three-quarters of a million dollars, I just can't see making such a concession to the feelings of the particular class of individuals who may happen to have more political influence than others.

Back: I can't either. But I'd like to carry my point a step farther, if I may.

One problem, as I see it, is whom are you going to defer? Where are you going to draw the line? Are you going to go out three miles and defer all this farm land; are you going to go out five miles; or whom are you going to defer?

Stocker: I had an answer to that in my paper.

Back: The second point is that you have the same problem that Mr. Ferraro described in his paper of farm land in Colorado—that it's all going up in value.

Vickrey: Yes, but I think the question to ask is, is the assessment justified by the income from the present use?

Anthony G. Ferraro: Income is only one factor in determining value.

Vickrey: Yes, but still, there is the farm land whose price is going up because some rich fellows who want tax deductions from their income tax are farming out in Virginia, say, in sort of a fashion—to raise horses or something. So all of this land is being bid up sky high. But there's the farmer who owns the land and is working it. There's really not much that he can do. He can sell out, to be sure, and if he's selling out because he prefers the money to having his farm, that's one thing. If he's forced to sell out because he can't raise the cash, that's another thing.

Now I think the fairly good criterion—I don't know how well it can be applied in the assessor's office—is simply to say that, of the value at which we have assessed the farm, this much is justified by the current earning power. The rest is future prospects or tax gimmicks or what have you, and it's on this difference that you allow the deferment.

House: When you talk about the deferred tax, I agree with you that deferral doesn't influence land use, at least I don't believe it does, in terms of the research that we have done.

Vickrey: It does in some cases. At least it influences land tenure and land use in the sense that Mr. X continues to farm rather than Mr. Y holding land as a speculation. It makes a change in land use; it may not change the day when a set of row houses begins to sprout up.

House: What I want to know is this: If taxes really do have some effect on land use, if we could say that giving the farmer a low tax would produce a better pattern of land use, would that provide society with a better reason for allowing a tax break?

Stocker: As a value judgment, I was only expressing my opinion as to the effectiveness this scheme would have.

But I would pick up one phrase you used and come back to the point that Mr. Vickrey was making, and that Mr. Back made, as to how far you go with the deferral. I don't see that there is any problem there. With deferral essentially you are not giving anything away. I can't conceive that there would be people clamoring to defer their taxes if you charge an appropriate rate of interest.

Back: It could be a real consideration in a particular budget year.

Stocker: I can't see except in very rare instances that this would account for a large part of your revenue.

Richard Lindholm: You could make a market for deferrals—develop a market for them and sell them to the bank. But I think that, if you are going to move to land value taxation, if you are going to emphasize it and move in this direction, you have to do everything you possibly can to make it easy to do. You need to do everything you can to reduce the various types of hardships that exist, and I don't know whether we put enough emphasis on the various procedures and methods of reducing the hardship when moving in this direction. I should certainly think that this would be one possibility—that you could make it somewhat easier to move more in this direction by deferral of tax with an appropriate interest charge. Not a cheap interest charge, and if there's a lot of inflation going on, go to higher interest, I mean a real market interest charge.

Back: I suppose so; nevertheless, if you are going into this game simply to take care of people who presumably are not able to pay their tax, I have much more sympathy for the retired person who still wants to maintain his home and doesn't have enough income to do it anymore and is forced to sell out because of high property taxes. The sympathy I have goes to the older people and not to this fellow sitting on a million dollars in the fringe areas of our cities.

Stocker: Let me say I think the principle of deferral of real estate taxes, with a lien being placed on the property, has opportunities for much wider application than that we have talked about here.

Realism: Character, Quality, and Limits of Ad Valorem Taxation

Lynn Anderson: I think we are dealing here with complex issues to which there are no simple pat answers. I am inclined to agree with Mr. Lindholm's remark that, if you are going to move in the direction of actually valuing land at its highest and best use, it is inevitable that we are to have a number of tax deferral schemes as necessary incentives. However, I do not foresee the day when the assessment of improvements will disappear.

We have, throughout this whole thing, a very complex situation of societal values clashing with one another; the economic development and efficiency point of view which would allocate this land to its highest and best use conflicts with emotional and sentimental attachments to land that Americans have and which you cannot overlook. You just do have concern for the older people and so forth.

Elsie Watters: One of the reasons I was interested in coming to this conference is that we have been thinking about doing something in the area of property taxation, which we have neglected too long at the Tax Foundation. I think some of the ideas we have picked up here will lead me to some productive lines of thought in that project.

As to the question of administrative obstacles to land value taxation, it occurs to me that there's no shortage of administrative obstacles to taxation of improvements. I don't know why administrative problems should provide any more of an obstacle to land value taxation as such.

Furthermore, it seems to me that there are tremendously more difficult variables operating in evaluation of improvements than there are in evaluation of land. Most of the administrative effort has been directed to assessment of improvements rather than to that of land.

Finally, I had one other point that I wanted to make. Some years ago I was exposed to a professor in the field of resources by the name of Eric Zimmerman. I suspect many of you remember or know of him. He had an expression: that there are resources versus neutral stuff. The point is that land *per se* is in the category of neutral stuff until you do something with it. There is no good basis for an abstract evaluation of land apart from what is done with it. This factor must always be considered in refining the assessment process.

Ferraro: Personally, I feel that most of the problems in the property tax field are more legislatively than administratively correctable. I think that somehow we need to rephrase the entire concept of property taxation.

I think we lose sight of the fact that we have an *ad valorem* principle. *Ad valorem* means exactly that to me. The value of the property is the tax base. Inability or ability to pay has nothing to do with *ad valorem* taxation. Now, if we don't like the property tax, I'd say abolish it, and let's talk about another tax. But as long as we are talking about this tax, I can't see how you can start making some of these proposed exceptions. You suggest preferential treatment for one man because you feel sorry that he can't afford to pay the tax even though he's got equity coming out his ears. Many people can't afford to pay. But I don't think ability to pay has anything to do with the *ad valorem* tax principle.

I also feel that in many cases we complicate the administrative process by getting involved in these extraneous fields.

Vickrey: I think it's worth noting that we were not talking about giving the taxpayer a break. We were talking about finding an easier way for the taxpayer to pay the same tax, and that's a very different thing.

Ferraro: Then you are adopting another tax criterion, ability to pay, which is quite different from our *ad valorem* base.

Vickrey: This is not a criterion that will affect what he or the property pays eventually. It's a matter of financing, not a matter of taxation. In effect, I have the tax to pay and it's hard for me to pay now, but I can pay it much more easily five years from now.

Ferraro: Then I suggest that, instead of preferential treatment, a Federal Homeowners' Bank Association or something of this nature be created where you can get a loan. But the process should not have any effect on the value of the property for taxation purposes.

Stocker: I don't see why society should deny itself a way of easing a problem that it feels it is facing for the sake of the alleged purity of some principle.

What happens if a tax deferral is granted? What kind of problems are created? Are there inequities created that are worse than the problems you solve? I think that's the way you have to evaluate this sort of policy proposal.

Ferraro: I think that, every time you alleviate somebody's problem, you create another problem of varying magnitude for the rest of society.

Stocker: We balance these.

Ferraro: Yes, you must.

Vickrey: No other taxpayer will have to pay a cent more because this fellow is granted a deferral.

Ferraro: But the higher the assessed valuation would be, the lower the tax burden proportion is for everybody. Therefore, in an ascendent society, instead of adding another $2,000,000 onto that tax roll and lowering a value or else supplying more services, you are in effect either cutting services or asking the rest of the taxpayers to foot your bill.

Vickrey: I disagree. First, we have the opportunity of banking these tax liens, if you want. So you don't have to——

Ferraro: That doesn't——

Vickrey: You can get the cash today from selling these tax liens.

Gaffney: If the tax collecting agency can do that, wouldn't it be better to have the taxpayer do it?

Vickrey: Of course. It's merely a question of what kind of an interest charge you can get. Now the tax collecting agency can go to the bank with a large number of these liens and get a better interest rate. The individual taxpayer with a first mortgage on his property can't go out and get a second mortgage for anything like that kind of rate of interest.

Gaffney: Forcing the taxpayer to pay a larger interest rate would encourage him to pay up immediately, and I suspect that nine times out of ten he can.

Vickrey: If he can, fine. There are cases where he can't.

Gaffney: These would probably be cases where the tax collecting agency would be assuming a considerable risk that it would never get paid by the taxpayer.

Stocker: If the lien is worth that little, if the lease associated with the lien is that great, then the man is probably overassessed.

Ferraro: I'd like to ask a question. What would be the administrative cost of processing these liens?

Vickrey: I don't think it would be very great. We have had a history of tax liens, and they have been dealt with on a large scale.

I appeal in this case to what's sometimes enunciated as Bogan's first law, which can be applied here and other places. Bogan's first law says that that which exists is possible. Land value taxation does exist in a number of jurisdictions; and if it does exist, I think this, according to Bogan's first law, shows that it's possible.

Gaffney: This tax lien is a euphemism, I think, for tax delinquency. Tax delinquency has a history of being resolved and paid later on at a very much scaled-down rate. I strongly suspect that very often the taxpayer never would pay, with or without interest, except at a compromised and reduced figure, and the rest of us would pick up the deficit.

Stocker: I don't think you can compare it, really, with tax delinquency. The typical situation in tax delinquency is that a property is declining in value, and the taxes themselves eat up a large part of the property and may exceed the value of the property. We are talking about a case in which typically the value of the property is rising.

Property Tax Progress

Alyea: I wonder if someone would like to comment upon other topics not yet covered today.

Ronald B. Welch: I wanted to say three things. First, lest some people get the impression that property tax administration is all bad, I wanted to say it really isn't as bad everywhere as it might seem from some of the criticisms made here. It really isn't the blind process that it might appear to be from some of the remarks that have been made; certainly we can't have self-assessment of a $3,000,000 plant as if its value were $600,000. We have a pretty respectable assessment process despite the fact we have had some bad eggs in the basket. The fact they came to light in California may indicate that we don't take errors and inequalities in assessment for granted quite as much as may be done in some other parts of the country.

Secondly, I wanted to say that I can agree with Mr. Back that you can administer a land value tax with a considerable degree of success. One of the reasons you can, in my opinion, is that you don't have much of a test of how poorly it is being administered since you have relatively few sales of land. You don't have nearly as many sales of bare land or land that is about to be bared by destruction of improvements as you do of real property generally. Therefore, the huge segment of your tax base remains untested as to the validity of your assessment. I would say, however, that your coefficient of dispersion for the properties where you do have a test is going to be higher. You'll have to recognize this as one of the things that will happen. You'll have coefficients which are perhaps three to four times as high as those we have now, because much of the land that you will be testing—that is, the bare land—is the hardest kind of property to assess. Your improvements are relatively easier to assess in many, many instances, since the great bulk are single-family residences. On land alone you are just bound to have high coefficients for what you can test. It doesn't mean that your valuations are unsatisfactory on the rest of your properties. You may be much better on the properties that you can't test than you are on those you can test. It does put state equalization action in a whole new context for every state except California and to a considerable extent for us as well because we have been using sales of real property as the test of the assessment level. So there needs to be developed some alternative. It could be state assessment or state assumption of the assessment process.

Weld Carter: On this second point of yours, I can conceive of a sale of land without any improvements on it, but I can't conceive of a sale in which there would be simply improvements with no land involved. It would seem to me, therefore, that every sale would have some land factor in it so that——

Welch: It has, but nobody knows what it is.

Carter: You have an assessment of land and improvements now.

Welch: You have only a guess as to what the land compo-
nent of a sale of improved property is. Now your assessor has
made the guess, but you have nothing to test his guess against
in the way of an actual markup phenomenon.

Vickrey: Not unless you have some class of property where
you can, with some reasonable reliability, think of depreciated
replacement cost as a measure of an improvement factor.

Welch: This is the way the assessors figure. I am looking for
some test of the assessor's efficiency. You test it by the same
process. Of course, somebody else can do the same thing he can
and come out with a different answer. Then you have two
judgments, one against the other.

Vickrey: I'm thinking you have a sale of a property which is
of a type that is generally not obsolescent and all the rest of it,
and then, when you take the depreciated value off for residual
land value and you test that sale against the assessment, it
won't be as good a test as the bare value.

Welch: It's not bad if you isolate those sales.

Carter: That's what you are doing now. It wouldn't be any
change.

Welch: We are not doing that in California as much as you
might think. Or maybe we are. I think I have jumped to a conclusion. What I meant to say is we are not using the so-called
summation approach very much in California or as much as
you think. We are using the sales approach and then breaking
the sale into two components, and we do break them the way
you say.

Administrative Problems No Bar to Property Tax
Policy Variation; Organizational Potentials

Back: Mr. Chairman, I wonder if we could change the subject, for this reason: I don't believe that this approach is the
answer to improving property tax administration. I think we'd
do just the opposite.

I have given a lot of thought to the question of how to improve property tax administration, and I believe the one key
place to begin is with organization. You are never going to

have good assessment administration when you have 2000 assessors as you have in Illinois, I believe, and perhaps 1000 in New Jersey. If you are looking at it overall, I think the first place to start is organization and getting primary assessing jurisdictions large enough to support a professional staff.

Alyea: Why not move all the way to the state?

Back: I would, since there's no reason why the tax base couldn't be determined by a higher level of government.

As I indicated in my paper, more and more of the states are going to the federal tax base for income tax purposes and applying their own rates. There's no reason why the technical professional job of establishing the property tax base shouldn't be done at a level of government high enough so that it can be done right.

Anderson: I agree with you. Here, again, you have one of the social conflicts that I was talking about, because this more centralized administration conflicts with the deep-seated American desire for grass-roots government at the lower level. You have to work these conflicts out, and you can no longer wait 100 years to do it.

Paul Corusy: Central assessment does not necessarily have to do with policy. All you have is a difficult administrative job to perform to find value. Conceptually it's as simple as that. It isn't home rule. People, I think, mix two separate things: home rule and local tax administration. In Illinois you could maintain local self-government just as well if technical assessment were done by fifty-five county assessors as you can now with assessment by 1230 township assessors.

I think this is the greatest problem there is today. You have to change the laws, and if you want improved administration, you'll get it if you change the laws.

Anderson: I agree with you 100 percent. I think Mr. Ferraro has made the point here. Administration is contingent upon improvement in the whole political climate and in the legislative process if you really want to get down to brass tacks. Tax administration doesn't exist in a vacuum independent of other facets of the political order.

Back: We are beginning piggyback sales taxes at the state

level. In Maryland we have a piggyback income tax at the local county level tied on to the state income tax. Perhaps the time will come when the state will determine the assessed values and let the local jurisdictions piggyback their rates on whatever rate the state applies.

Vickrey: I might try to bring the discussion back to the problem of land value taxation, and I would like to raise the question whether land value taxation as defined in strict economic terms is precisely the objective that we want. The objectives and consequences that we expect from land value taxation are basically that the tax is to be independent of improvements so as to eliminate the dragging of tax on improvements. This leads to the thought that any kind of tax that is substantially independent of the value of the improvements on the individual lot will accomplish this purpose whether or not it happens to coincide with some economist's definition of what land value is. I would also make the comment that, if you adhere strictly to land value taxation in the economic conceptual sense, you may find that land values are quite erratic both geographically and over time in terms of what land developers have done either to overdevelop or to underdevelop the land, especially if you have an area in which land is pretty built up and you find that there are new and higher uses that are needed and for which no vacant land has been reserved. Then you've got to demolish a residence which may be in fairly good shape, and the cost of land in that entire area then becomes the value of the land plus the improvement.

On the other hand, if there has been some offer through speculation and a lot of vacant land has been held for better uses and it turns out that more land has been held for this purpose than is going to be developed in this higher and better use, then the land may become a drug on the market, and you may have people in rather comparable circumstances paying very substantially different taxes simply on the basis of the fancies of speculators over the past ten- or twenty-year period.

Now I suspect that it may be possible to develop theories of what I won't call land value taxation but rather "improvement-independent-taxation of real estate" that might determine a way of distributing the tax burden which would still be independent of what a person does by way of improving his own land but which would not be too offensive against notions of equity.

We were talking earlier about the possibility of deriving an assessment which might or might not pretend to be a land value—that is, an assessment base which would be simply the taking of the properties within a given radius of a given property and finding out the total value of improvements of such properties. Perhaps two or three rings with different radii could be selected and a formula applied which would determine a "land value" or a pseudo-land value for a particular piece of property, a value which would be developed from the aggregate of improvements on the land itself and adjacent land.

Arthur P. Becker: Aren't you stressing improvement unduly, though? People might want to value this land for the space that it gives.

Vickrey: I am not saying that this would in all cases correspond to a proper assessment of land value. Obviously, if you get a choice residential plot that is located in a finger of residential land jutting into a golf course, this will be very highly valuable land, but according to the improvement criterion it would have a low assessment. I am not saying that this would correspond to our notions of land value taxation, but I think cases in which you'd have such inequities would be relatively few; and if the tax base is fairly easily ascertainable and definite, the tax base gets capitalized into the land value and a good deal of the inequity is taken out of it.

Becker: What you are really driving at is a concept of a workable or normal land value rather than one that is predominantly precise.

Vickrey: I am not saying the rule I propose is the only one; but when one says "land value taxation," what one is really after is not, *per se* and for its own sake, the taxation of what is economically defined as land value. Your objectives are really defined operationally somewhat differently. You want the assessment to be independent of your own improvements and from the point of allocation of resources.

Gaffney: I think there is an operational analogy. What you are suggesting is similar to agricultural rents; county average yields are often used in setting rents on individual properties. However, to the extent that your proposal suggests taking the building either on an individual site or on a collection of sites as an index to the land value, with the thought that they tend to be proportional to each other, I think there is a very real danger of going astray because a building is not income. It represents cost, and land value is what is left over after cost. Buildings can really represent a net detraction from land value if it takes a lot of building to get a given income. I think there is a danger of taking marginal land that has no value after cost and putting a high assessment on it if you take buildings as an index to the value of the land underneath them. You could have land that is marginal, not because of low yields but because of high costs, which, under this kind of scheme, would be assessed at a high rate.

Vickrey: Yes. If you own a swamp that is next door to one of those hotels in the woods, it might be impractical to build on it, and you wouldn't want to assess the swamp simply as a tribute to a value created by the value of the proximity of the hotel.

Becker: If you have another potential developer there, according to Arch Woodruff, it would be all right to assess it.

Arthur D. Lynn, Jr.: One would have to observe that the litigation possibilities in this tax proposal are by no means insignificant. If you transfer the value from a hotel owner to the swamp owner and then tax the swamp owner on that unrealized and not-in-fact-transferred augmentation of value attributable to the hotel, I should think he would go see his friendly legal counselor.

Vickrey: I just threw out that somewhat off-the-cuff suggestion to indicate that the pure concept of land value may not be what we are looking for.

Gaffney: Putting it more generally, I would say that there are classes of land value and that the ratio of optimal improvement to land value is very different from class to class. In industry, for example, the ratio of improvement value to land value tends to be very high. In garbage dumps, it is the other way around. There are land-using uses. There are capital-using uses.

Lindholm: When I think of administration of this land value taxation, I come up with the idea that you should move toward the contract city with respect to taxation of improvements and toward taxation of land as a source of state revenues, allocated with equal rate around the state.

If we can move toward thinking of land and its taxation in a different fashion from the taxation of buildings and improvements, and if we can begin relating improvements directly to the services of the contract city while leaving taxation of land at the state level, then we would have uniform land taxes wherever the land is owned, on the basis of its value. Administratively and conceptually, there would be many advantages to this pattern. Tax change could move toward the separation of land value from the value of the structure and thus permit development of some of the basic ideas in land value taxation.

Welch: It seems to me that what you are suggesting would require at least state administration of the assessment of land because of the difficulty of imposing a state tax on property subject to variable local assessment. You will recall that historic difficulties with this matter resulted in the old separation of revenue sources idea. It seems to me you would have to have state administration of your proposal.

Alyea: Would you object to state administration of land?

Welch: It's a pretty formidable problem in a state like California. I can see it easily in a state like Rhode Island or Delaware; but when you think of 6,000,000 parcels of land in a state with as many square miles of territory as California, it's kind of frightening. You would have to have a huge organization, highly decentralized, and while I am not prepared to say you couldn't do as good a job of administration or better, perhaps, I do say it would be a tremendous task to get started.

Lynn: I think that this is a good point for me to call a halt to these proceedings. Messrs. Back and Becker have said that we have the administrative capacity successfully to levy a land value tax when and if the tax policy makers decide to adopt such an impost. Mr. Welch has noted that there would be great difficulty in measuring the degree of success in such taxation but the very difficulty may be a positive advantage. Mr. Vickrey has reminded us that there are several different alternative tax means in land value taxation. The consensus of this conference is that land value taxation need not be barred by purely administrative concerns. Nevertheless, much remains to be done by way of demonstrating how land can be most accurately and effectively assessed for tax purposes. The assessment of land values would be a most appropriate topic for a future conference.

Index